A HISTORY OF SURREY

Ham House, North Drawing Room.

THE DARWEN COUNTY HISTORY SERIES

A History of Surrey

PETER BRANDON

Drawings by Carolyn Lockwood

PHILLIMORE

First published 1977

by

PHILLIMORE & CO., LTD.,

London and Chichester

Head Office: Shopwyke Hall

Chichester, Sussex, England

ISBN 0 85033 303 2

Printed in England by

UNWIN BROTHERS, LTD.,

at The Gresham Press, Old Woking, Surrey

and bound by

THE NEWDIGATE PRESS LTD.,

at Book House, Dorking, Surrey

Contents

This book is dedicated to
the memory of
Edward Thomas, killed at Arras, 1917,
author of *The South Country* (1909) and many other
works of natural history

'Some day there will be a history of England written from the point of view of one parish, or town, or great house . . . It will begin with a geological picture, something large, clear, architectural, not a mass of insignificant names. It must be imaginative; it might, perhaps lean sometimes upon Mr. Doughty's *Dawn in Britain*. The peculiar combination of soil and woodland and water determines the direction and position and importance of the ancient trackways; it will determine also the position and size of human settlements. The early marks of these—the old flint and metal implements, the tombs, the sight of agriculture, the encampments, the dwellings—will have to be clearly described and interpreted. Folk-lore, legend, place-names must be learnedly, but bravely and humanly used, so that the historian who has not the extensive sympathy and imagination of a great novelist will have no chance of success. What endless opportunities will he have for really giving the feel of past times in such matters as the line made by the edge of an old wood with the cultivated land, the shapes of the fields with their borders of streams or hedge or copse or pond or wall or road, the purpose and interweaving of the roads and footpaths. . . . Architecture, with many of its local characteristics still to be traced, will speak as a voice out of the stone of castle, church, manor, farm, barn and bridge. The birds and beasts cannot be left out. The names of the local families—gentle and simple— what histories are in them in the curt parish registers, in tombstones, in the names of fields and houses and woods'.

Surrey parkland

The South Country, p. 152.

6

Maps and Plans

*Holmdale, the home of
the architect G. E. Street*

*'Not wholly in the busy world, nor quite
Beyond it, blooms the garden that I love.'*

*Richmond Hill, (by E.
Radclyffe after T. Allom),
early nineteenth century*

List of Illustrations

Acknowledgements

The author is grateful to the following for permission to reproduce illustrations: Trustees of the British Museum, nos. 3, 8, 10, 18; *Country Life*, nos. 22, 30, 31; Christ Church College, Oxford, no. 20; Downing Street Studios, Farnham, no. 25; London Borough of Merton, Library Services, nos. 11, 24, 27, 33, 34, 36, 37; Minet Library, London Borough of Lambeth, nos. 28, 42, 43, 45; the Public Record Office, London, nos. 9, 10; Richmond Public Library, nos. 16, 17; the *Österreichische Nationalbibliothek*, Vienna, nos. 13, 14; Robin Skinner, no. 4; Southern Air Photographs, Guildford, no. 48; The Tate Gallery, London, nos. 1, 38; *The Times*, no. 47; The Victoria and Albert Museum, no. 15; The Walker Art Gallery, Liverpool, no. 2; Picturepoint Ltd., no. 40. The other photographs are by the author.

My warm thanks go to the staff of the County Record Offices at Guildford and Kingston, the Minet Library, Brixton, and of the library, Merton College, Oxford. To Elizabeth Dawlings and Robin Skinner, of the Department of Geography, The Polytechnic of North London, I am greatly indebted for cartography and photography respectively. Mrs. Ann Ollis, of the same department, provided indispensable support. I am pleased also to acknowledge the great help of Ann Winser, Site Librarian, The Polytechnic of North London, who provided the index and helped to clarify expression. To Noel Osborne, Editorial Director of Phillimore, I wish to record my sincere gratitude for his friendly help, advice and encouragement.

A special debt is owed to Mrs. Myfanwy Thomas and Prof. R. George Thomas for permission to dedicate this book to the memory of Surrey-born Edward Thomas.

I Surrey's Green Mantle

In this book it is proposed to take the county boundary as it stood before 1888 when metropolitan Surrey was removed to form part of the new county of London. For many centuries this historic county of Surrey has borne the dual character of the Londoner's pleasure resort and his much sought-after place of residence. The huge predominance of a modern city is found even in the county's remotest corners for professional and business men have by preference long moved westwards out of London in search of fresh air and a garden. The ever-expanding influence of London has made Surrey the residential appendage of an over-grown monster of a city, the largest the world had ever seen in 1900. This has wrought much social and landscape disruption. So compelling has been the social *cachet* of a Surrey home that the part of the county nearest the metropolis has been overrun by a London-drawn population, and the whole county has become permeated with London's dynamism and life-style. Much of Surrey has been blotted out completely and the continuing spread of population from a major world city puts its remaining countryside of great beauty and immense historic value under constant threat of similar oblivion. Only by checking London's outward growth by successively more widely-drawn extensions of the Green Belt concept, and the ceaseless vigilance of many individuals and national bodies concerned with preserving rural England, has Surrey been saved. The county is still a battleground for an intense struggle between town and country, making it a planner's problem region. At stake are the still extensive open spaces which long defied the plough and are now seen as one of Surrey's chief glories, offering welcome relaxation for those who snatch a few hours from the noisy and congested streets of inner and suburban London.

The face of Surrey vividly records the effects of these forces for change. As the old county of Surrey slips past a suburban train window, hillsides striped by endless rows of red- and grey-roofed houses fill the view. At about the eighth milestone from the busy exits of Waterloo and Victoria, the traveller is conscious of a blurred vision of imitation Tudor semi-detached houses, indistinguishable from the suburbs of Wembley or the Great West Road. A distance of 12 miles from central London brings one to the inner edge of the 'Stockbroker Belt', a type of landscape born of our own era, neither town nor

Ashurst Rough, Box Hill

11

Huntsman (Ms. Bodley 546)

country. Large houses sprawl across former fields and along once-deserted lanes and lie embedded in pylon-bisected playing fields, immaculately-groomed golf courses, riding schools and hospitals. This is the land of the businessman's dreams but in order to mould it nearer to his heart's desire he has unwittingly shattered its former charm and turned the country into something like one vast town.

Nevertheless, the inheritance from Surrey's long process of formation and self-development is altogether richer than the foregoing description suggests. Although there has probably never been a time when it was not geographically an extension of London, Surrey has had until comparatively recently a distinct society and way of life. Even today, the majority of its working inhabitants are not London commuters but residents of one of the many historic and in part still beautiful Surrey towns. From an airliner landing at Gatwick, or observed from one of the county's many choice viewpoints, a cultivated landscape of an exquisitely varied surface spreads in far-extended shades of green. 'Nowhere in England is richer foliage, or wilder downs and fresher woodlands', wrote George Meredith (1828–1909) as recently as 1882, to whom they were the very substance of his poetry and many of his novels. His statement is happily still generally true for numerous relatively untamed places still survive in Surrey as unspoilt as any now left in England. More than 4,000 years have gone into the making of this rural landscape. Men first cleared woodlands, drained marshes and reclaimed heaths. They built houses, shaped fields, wore down trackways. They have sown and reaped a thousand or more crops in fields which we now hold in trust for those who will follow. In so doing they turned a once savage wilderness into a landscape so little like the wild that Surrey has long been regarded as part of the Garden of England. Few parts of England have been so zealously and affectionately manicured. This has imbued the surviving rural face of Surrey with the polished and mellow appearance which makes it still commonly regarded as one of the finest environments near London in which to live and work (Plates 1, 2 and 4).

Surrey agriculture has never made a major contribution to the national wealth on account of difficulties of the soils which are discussed more fully in Chapter IV. No wide stretches of waving corn fill the Surrey landscape. Indeed, a considerable part was very scantily populated until a continuous stream of wealth was pumped in from prosperous metropolitan sources. We first discern this in the early middle ages when Surrey was a place of huntsmen and warriors and its main function in national life was to offer relaxation within easy reach of London, as innumerable medieval forests, chases and parks are witnesses. Some of the finest hunting was afforded by the thickly-

Huntsman (Ms. Bodley 546)

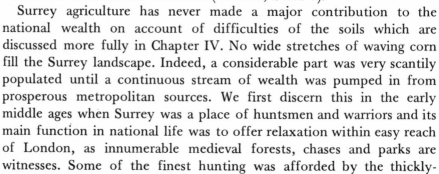

12

wooded and well-hedged country of the central North Downs and the adjoining Vale of Holmesdale between the rivers Mole and Medway, where *c.* 1200 the game comprised fox, hare, partridge and pheasant, as well as the woodland cat (*felis sylvestris*). So highly prized were these Surrey sporting amenities that the Crown claimed that the whole of Surrey was within Forest Law. By the 15th century wealthy London merchants had become interested in Surrey real estate and came to retire as landowners, portentous of everything to come. Their monumental brass effigies in civilian dress are distinctive features of Surrey churches—for example, of Bletchingley, Farleigh and Mickleham. Sixteenth-century civilians also commemorated by Surrey brasses include a number of officials of the royal households of Nonesuch, Sheen, Oatlands and Hampton Court, public officers such as sheriffs, keepers of royal parks and a numerous group of City businessmen. Engraved in a close-fitting medieval tunic or in the ruff and doublet fashionable in the 16th century, these brasses are proof of the steadily-increasing place in Surrey life of immigrants connected with the political, legal and commercial life of the nation.

Monumental brass of a civilian, Horley, c.1510

From the 17th century the face of Surrey has also been repeatedly reshaped by successive generations striving to achieve ideal forms of landscape. Early 18th-century travellers contemplating scenery were predisposed towards undulating country where the complete humanisation of nature has imparted to the landscape many of the virtues conventionally ascribed to a garden. The soft, garden-like quality of the Surrey scene (excluding its heaths and the higher parts of the bare Downs) conformed to this conventionally accepted notion of the beautiful, and ever since its quiet and shapely lines have attracted general admiration. Consequently Surrey came to be esteemed as a district where garden-like scenery could be created cheaply and perfectly. Surrey's wilder hilly and heathy tracts were not aesthetically appreciated until the impulse of the Romantic and Picturesque movement towards the end of the 18th century. With the growing predeliction for such 'wild' places, these parts of the county were being colonised in the later part of the 19th century by people intent on playing the rôle of country gentry.

This reshaped scenery in parks, gardens and arboreta has imparted to Surrey some of the finest works of landscape art. Much of this brilliantly creative landscaping was extended to farmland on the principle of beauty-in-use and the spread of this artistic endeavour turned many Surrey estates, in the words of Christopher Hussey, into a 'vast created landscape natural enough to our eyes but in reality managed as much for picturesque appearance as for economic returns'. This delicate balance between pleasure and utility has now been aban-

13

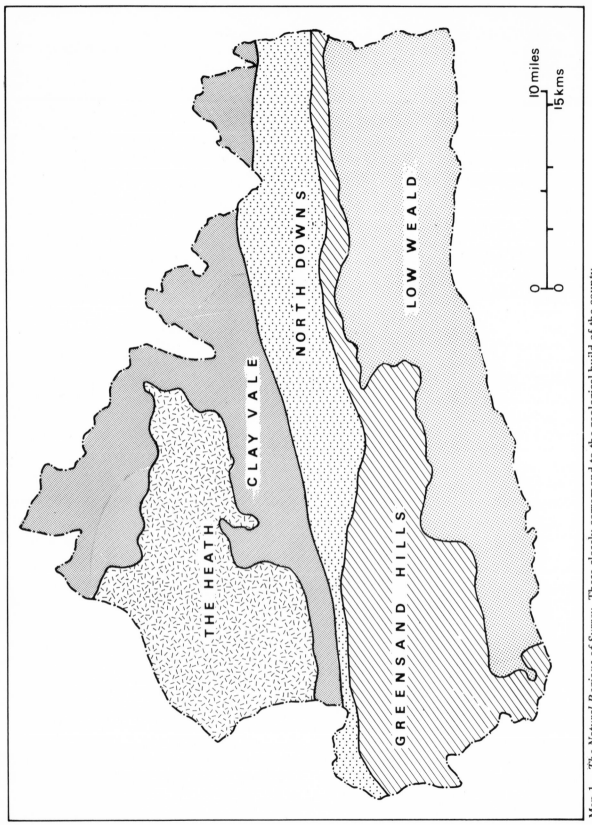

Map 1. *The Natural Regions of Surrey.* These closely correspond to the geological build of the county.

doned and leaves the unanswered question as to how the best of this landscape heritage is to be properly conserved.

Before the Enclosures and the Industrial Revolution stamped out local crafts and industry, Surrey was also an important manufacturing county. As early as the 13th century its peasants were deeply involved in craft activities. The scattered forest hamlets of the Weald, in particular, were alive with business, full of artisans supplementing their hard-won living from the land with various forms of by-employment. They grappled with local raw materials such as timber, clay, iron, water, wool, hides and sand (for glass-making). Evidence of woodcrafts such as coopering, turnery and tanning is well preserved by the names of persons listed in medieval documents by surnames derived from their trade, such as William *le Cupere*; surnames such as Fuller (a cloth finisher by trade) or Smith (used of an ironworker as well as a black-smith) are also common. By the 16th and 17th centuries the west Surrey rivers of the Wey, Tillingbourne and Mole were harnessed to provide motive power to work mills making iron, brass, cloth, paper and gunpowder. Many of these mills survived until the late 19th century as flour or grist mills.

Medieval smith, from an illuminated Ms.

These activities of man in Surrey have been played out in a landscape which is the joint product of man and nature. Its essence is a remarkable variety of surface. Although one of the smaller English counties, thinking of Surrey one recalls to mind not one landscape but a mosaic of four—the still densely wooded Weald; the wild, rough, sweeps of heathland around Hindhead and Leith Hill; the Chalk upland of the North Downs; and the quiet, reposeful vales which interweave the other landscapes together. Surrey is rich in strong and unexpected contrasts because its geology is unusually varied over short distances. The key factor in these differences from a farming point of view was the workability of the soils. This ranged from ease of working on sandy loams on which it is not difficult to keep a plough straight, to considerable difficulty on the dry, thin, flinty Chalk soils, which caused the plough to jump and every nerve to be strained in keeping a furrow; and the impossibility of ploughing the cold, wet, unkind Wealden clays, except in favourable weather. There were also, as will be more fully explained later, important differences in inherent soil fertility. Thus each of the comparatively small contrasting soil regions in Surrey, corresponding to 'pays' in France, set different conditions for human use. One of the main themes of this history is the play of the economic, social and cultural forces on each of these regions, so producing their differing, and at times, divergent development. In tracing their history we feel the strength of natural forces that shaped peoples' lives and the human energy with which they shaped their local landscape.

15

Old timber houses, Lingfield

This reconciliation between man and land in Surrey was worked out over an experience of many centuries and by the late 18th century its exceptionally variegated scenery was exerting a strong fascination upon the artist, the musical composer, the man of letters, and the naturalist. It was quick, complete changes of scenery that led the artist J. M. W. Turner (1775–1851) into his frenzied drawing activity. In the course of his many journeys across Surrey to Petworth House, the home of his patron, Lord Egremont, he sensed and recreated the faint but palpable tang of wildness still evident in the Surrey woodland. Numerous of his pencil sketches preserved in many notebooks record his visual pleasure at glimpses of the varied and richly-wooded Surrey landscape where 'at every turn some fresh picture opened upon us'. He never ceased to search the Weald for tree groups, as in the lovely river Wey gap at Guildford, or the changing mood of Wealden skies and, with a keen miniaturist's eye, he swiftly sketched the Wealdsman —whether carter, hedger, ploughman or woodman—and his doings. His sketchbooks unravel with a freshness and accuracy matched only by William Cobbett's virile prose, many contryside events of a kind which are rarely the concern of written records. It is a common error to suppose that history must be something written down (Plate 3).

Surrey scenery was also an inspiration to George Meredith who devoted his imagination, half Celtic, half Saxon, to the praise of the Surrey landscape and whose poems 'The Orchard and the Heath' and the 'Night Walker' record the scenic variations in a day's walk. Samuel Palmer (1805–1881), an artist now at last gaining public esteem, revelled in riding along the line where the uncultivated heaths and woods of the 'wild' gave way to garden-like fields and orchards, one of the most characteristic west Surrey landscape features. William Cobbett (1762–1835), whose ability to infer the influence exerted by the sub-soil on surface cultivation has probably never been equalled, has expressed this scenic variety in agricultural terms: 'The county of Surrey presents to the eye of the traveller a greater contrast than any other county in England. It has some of the very best and some of the worst lands, not only in England, but in the world'. In a rare record of his aesthetic contentment he also penned a word picture of the diverse country of the Wey valley between Godalming and Guildford: 'Here are hill and dell in endless variety. Here are Chalk and sand, vieing with each other in making beautiful scenes. Here are woods and downs. Here is something of everything but fat marshes and those skeleton-making agues'. It is this upper valley of the Wey, which Cobbett considered the most agreeable and 'happy-looking' he had ever seen, that brings all Surrey together, both the rich alluvial and valley land and the intermingled poorer land on the Chalk and Lower Greensand

1. John Linnell's *Noonday Rest* (1865). The vast bowl of space which is the Wealden landscape has captured the imagination of successive generations of artists since John Constable declared the prospect was the most sublime he had ever experienced.

2. John Brett's *The Stonebreaker* (1865) is a good example of intensive and patient observation of Box Hill, the Vale of Mickleham and the distant Weald.

3. The Wey gap at Guildford. A page from J. M. W. Turner's sketchbook.

4. Juniper Bottom, (George Meredith's 'Happy Valley') one of a number of delightful dry Chalk valleys which lead from Box Hill to White Hill.

formations. In many ways this little district between Milford and Guildford is the core and centre of the richly complex world of old Surrey, the county's cradle, so to speak, and a microcosm of the whole. Here we find evidence of relatively dense prehistoric settlement, and of later pagan Saxons worshipping idols in the woodland groves, the first Surrey towns, and a flourishing medieval cloth industry. Near our own time, its scenery and buildings visibly inspired Gertrude Jekyll to create new styles of garden design and the same corner of Surrey had an imporant influence upon the career of Edwin Lutyens, the architect. The meeting of the contrasting landscapes in this district appears to have been a stimulus to observation and artistic creativity (for, in addition to Jekyll and Lutyens, William Cobbett and Gilbert White, the Selborne naturalist, have brought it fame) (Map 1, p. 14).

Viewed from the Sussex Downs and Leith Hill, which command magnificent panoramas, or from a similar distance afar, the Weald presents to the eye the appearance of a fertile and rich country. This impression is a false one. The Weald Clay supports a luxuriant growth of trees and shrubs, especially oak, but the wood-clearing Saxons who moved in to wrest fields from the forest found it a hard land to win and a hard land to hold. The soils are tenacious and thus difficult to plough in adverse seasons and they require large artificial increases in manure. It was the imperious necessity of new land for a growing population which brought into existence raw, unfinished communities in the woodland clearings attached to parent centres in the older settled Vale of Holmesdale and still further north. These men who first laid the Weald bare for cultivation were as much pioneers of human settlement as the backwoodsmen who penetrated the more distant parts of North America many centuries later. Unknown families, apparently between the 8th or 9th and 13th centuries, generation by generation, set their hands to the centuries-long task of taming the Surrey Weald and applied the strength and ardour of their life without stint or limit in a slow, painful battle forward, little by little, towards a life of increasing comfort and wealth. The Wealden forest, long a 'wood beyond the world', then echoed to the ringing sound of the sharp and measured strokes of the pioneer's axe; thousands of trees were hewn down and the homes of countless wild beasts and birds destroyed by men selecting sites for homes and fields. As the forest receded, streams grew shallower and muddier, and some ran dry. This winning of new land from the forest was the achievement of small-holding forest dwellers—hard, bold, sturdy, unsophisticated, and as strong as the soil they worked upon. In plying their axes to clear patches of the forest and to fence off a few acres round their rough huts they had to learn new ways of living from those

Medieval swineherd (Corpus Christi Coll. 285)

17

practised on the older settled parts of Surrey developed on more favourable soils, whence they had come. Amongst new skills they acquired were forestry and woodcrafts, for the forest dwellers soon learned that trees were the best crop on the heaviest clays for bad times and wet seasons did not touch the Surrey woods.

The later history of man's occupation of the Weald is marked by recurrent setbacks in which the economy stagnated or even retrogressed and the human community was at bay, shrunk within itself, amidst a rural landscape collapsing into dereliction. Such periods of adversity are interspersed between more prosperous and stable ones. Examples of 'lean' years are several runs of bad seasons between 1300 and 1480; the recession following the decline of the charcoal iron industry at the end of the 17th century; the dismal 1830s, 1870s, and 1930s. Conversely, the 'fat' years of the mid–13th century, the early 1600s and the Napoleonic Wars (1793–1820) are also readily identifiable.

In north-west Surrey the salient feature of the landscape before the early 19th century was the great sand-waste on the sterile soils of the Bagshot formation. This consisted almost entirely of sand covered with heather and fern, and studded with large peat-bottomed meres and marshes on impervious ironstone layers. The boggy patches, haunted by myriads of wild fowl, were still called 'moors' by the local folk as late as the last century from a word derived from Old English *mora,* a bog. The reclamation of these heathlands played an important part in the development of a regional peasant society in Surrey. It was by far the worst land in Surrey from which medieval man produced his daily bread. With no deep rich soil at their disposal peasants burned and tore up the broom, gorse and heather to make fields, and dried out marshy hollows. The heath gradually shrank before the efforts of land-hungry peasants in the 13th and early 14th centuries by which time virtually all the better land, including that of the Weald, had previously been brought to agricultural use. Most of this former wild lay within the Royal Forest of Windsor or was held by the great Abbeys of Chertsey and Westminster, both of which had received large grants of the waste. Despite the need for more farmland, the sterility of the sands made reclamation slow and difficult, and after the heavy mortality of the Black Death in 1348 many enclosures reverted to waste and were not again improved until the 17th century.

Even as late as 1830 large tracts of the sand-waste remaining survived unmastered, 'unscarred by a single human dwelling, scarcely changing from century to century', for the soil was too poor to have tempted reclamation on any large scale. In the 1850s travellers by the Southampton railway were astonished to find themselves 'whirling through miles of desert' within an hour's travelling distance of London

A two-bay cottar's single storey cottage, originally wattle and daub with a thatched roof, Chobham. After Surrey Vernacular Architecture Group

18

and in sight of only the little holdings of squatter families, locally known as 'broom squires', considered the most primitive form of rural society in Surrey. By the late 19th century the Surrey heaths were coming into the hands of builders. The realisation that the soil conditions of acid podsols on the heaths closely resembled the native soils of increasingly popular imported American and Himalayan shrubs, together with the cheapness and suitability of heathland for building, imparted the conviction that 'pine country' within commuting distance of London gave 'real and abiding advantages for modern country life'. The late Victorian middle class was seized with such a compelling perception of 'pine country' as providing the best soil, the purest air and the healthiest surroundings that the 'rush to the pine woods' in the wild and previously almost undiscovered corners of Surrey became a minor urban exodus.

Wall with garneted joints, a typical form of west Surrey decoration. The black pieces of stone inserted in the mortar are fragments of local ironstone

On the north of the little vale of the river Wey, which is continued eastwards across Surrey as the Vale of Holmesdale, the North Downs rise suddenly and steeply like a spine. The boldest of these hills—often in the past called 'Chalk-pit Hills' because half the mortar of London and countless loads of lime for Surrey crops was scooped out of their gleaming white hillsides—is White Hill, near Caterham. The highest crests and much of the gravelly drift on their flanks supported only thin, penurious soils, which from the 17th century have been progressively improved under the stimulus of London's increasing food market. On these summits was for centuries the sheep walk which brought prosperity in the form of the cloth industry to the towns and villages at their feet. The Vale was formerly the most heavily populated part of Surrey. Its tightly-clustered villages (though they had shrunk before recent modern growth) and fine examples of half-timbered houses are tokens of this fomer prosperity. Camden's comment that its intermixture of woods, fields and meadows renders the landscape 'exceeding pleasant' is a reminder that the Elizabethan taste for such scenery was much the same as our own.

The 'hollow' lanes which lead from the vale villages up on to the rough heaths of the Leith Hill mass or to the crests of the Downs lend distinctive charm to this district. They twist their way many feet below the surface of the surrounding fields, grotesquely worn out of the soft rocks of the Upper and Lower Greensand strata by the combined action of the fretting or rain and age-long traffic or of the bursting out of one of the many Surrey springs. Gilbert White (1720–1793) was the first to comment on these beautiful features. They still remain, as in his day, rich collections of flora and wild life, but they are less subject to flooding (because of controlled under-field drainage) and the severe frosts which added wildness in his day.

19

II Before the Saxons

Man's record in Surrey extends over more than 500,000 years, but not until agriculture was introduced about 3,000 B.C. did he leave any recognisable earthworks in the present landscape. Over most of this vast span of time man struggled for survival between successive ice sheets. During the warmer periods called interglacials, human groups moved northwards from Europe and became hunters. Man learned to build himself a shelter and to make fire; to clothe himself and to transmit ideas in speech and by cave paintings. In these ways, and by his superior tool-making ability, he slowly emerged from the status of an animal. The reconstruction of Palaeolithic man's land surface is difficult because much of it has been obliterated by subsequent weathering and erosion and by the waste deposited on it as river gravels in the valleys. The oldest humanly-made implements found in Surrey are the Eoliths, crude borers and scrapers, found buried in the gravels of the river Wey near Farnham and Guildford. Later in his evolution man made flint hand-axes termed Palaeoliths. Unfortunately, modern gravel extraction now uses mechanical methods instead of hand digging and this has greatly reduced the chances of finds of ancient man.

Palaeolithic hand-axe

The Mesolithic nomads who wandered westwards across Europe in the new territories opened up for habitation by the increasing warmth between *c.* 10,000–4,000 B.C. are well represented in Surrey. These people were still at the mercy of their environment. They dwelt typically beside streams or meres on patches of lightly-wooded ground interrupting the great spread of prevailing deciduous forest then covering 'Surrey', subsisting on deer, fish and fowl. The most favourable food-gathering environment in Surrey was the Chalk-bounded heaths on the Lower Greensand formation, dissected by streams and meres. This area of south-west Surrey has yielded more evidence of Mesolithic occupation than any other district of South-East England. (Map 2, p. 21). Its most characteristic legacy in the landscape is the chipping-floor where flint derived from the North Downs was prepared by flaking into flint-points for arrow shafts, knives, saws, gouges and scrapers. The many thousands of such implements collected from the Surrey heaths is evidence of intense hunting activity; one site has yielded more than 85,000 artifacts, mostly waste flakes produced in making small-worked flints called microliths. One Mesolithic site is of particular significance and interest. It is at Abinger Farm Manor,

20

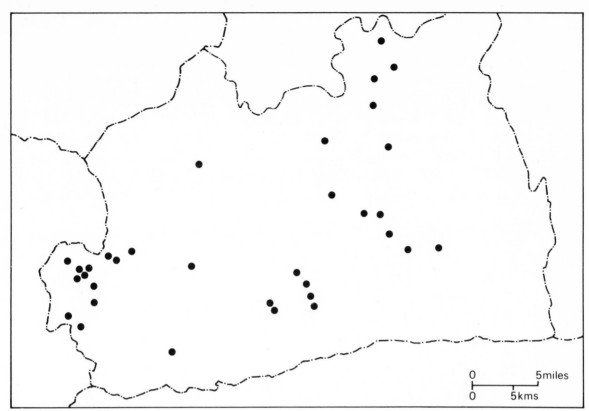

Map 2a. The Mesolithic occupation of Surrey. After W. F. Rankine, *The Mesolithic of South England*, Surrey Archaeological Research Paper No. 4 (1956).

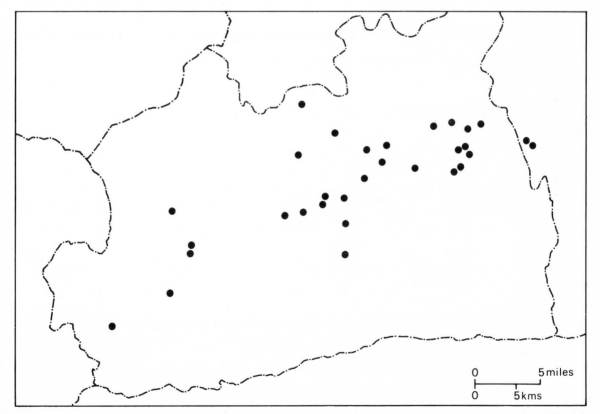

Map 2b. The early Anglo-Saxon burial sites. After Audrey Meaney, *A gazetteer of early Anglo Saxon burial sites* (1964).

Mesolithic axes (after Rankine)

close by one of the natural springs so characteristic of Surrey. Here Dr. L. S. B. Leakey, responsible for the famous discoveries of ancient man in Kenya, excavated the pit dwelling deemed to be the oldest humanly-made and preserved dwelling in Britain. It is a shallow pit scooped out of the soft sandstone by means of sharpened wooden stakes or deer antlers. Along one side is a ledge, probably a sleeping bench. Post holes mark the position of supports for a simple sloping roof of bracken and skins. A pile of stones may indicate the hearth area.

The new era in Britain which began before 3,000 B.C. with the arrival from the continent of the Neolithic peoples who brought the inventions of agriculture and the art of pottery, flint-mining and trade, is poorly authenticated in Surrey. Future excavation can be expected to fill in some of the gaps in our knowledge. On the basis of our existing information there seems little evidence that the culturally advanced Neolithic people who settled in the better endowed parts of Southern England greatly extended their influence to Surrey, where the people practised no doubt a certain amount of farming, but also their old habits of hunting and gathering. Ancient man was coming to terms with the reality of his Surrey habitat. He had to make the best of conditions as he found them and he learnt to arrange his life to suit them. By the third millennium B.C. these people were probably exploiting the downland by clearing the scrub by means of flint hand-axes and fire and extending the cultivation of wheat and barley, together with the husbandry of sheep and cattle. They would have chosen the more lightly wooded areas for settlement. Many parts of the Downs are plastered with Clay-with-Flints, probably supporting a dense cover of oak and beech which would doubtless have required much effort and the heavier iron axes of the Iron Age for its clearance.

It is in the Neolithic period that the dual North Downs trackway probably first came into use. This lay in a narrow corridor between the forested Weald and the also heavily wooded Vale of the Thames sloping northwards, and it provided access between the more desirable habitation sites of early men in Wiltshire and those on the channel coast of Kent and Sussex. Known as the Harrow Way in Hampshire and the Pilgrim's Way in Surrey, it forms a continuous trackway at the foot of the Chalk escarpment. This was probably a 'winter' route for the chalky soils were relatively dry. This lower route is duplicated by a ridge-way which would have afforded easier going than the Pilgrim's Way when the heavy mire dried out in summer. Yet another ridgeway is provided by a branch running along the line of the Lower Greensand hills between St. Martha's and Seale.

For the more sophisticated fitting of the economy to natural resources which is the hallmark of the Bronze and Iron Ages in

22

Southern Britain, the picture for Surrey is very incomplete, especially concerning the wider social and economic contexts of the settlements. The whole organisation of the landscape and problems of arable and pastoral use of the land in relation to settlement, livestock, water supply and woodland management have still to be worked out. The comparative scarcity of recorded sites of human habitation compared with the Chalk areas of Kent and Sussex may be genuine, but it could also be partly explained at least by the much less widespread investigation of antiquity made in Surrey than in neighbouring counties. Archaeologists are now showing in other previously neglected areas such as the upper Thames valley in Oxfordshire and Berkshire that prehistoric settlement may have been rather different in character and with a rather more complex economy than on the better-known Chalklands. For Surrey our knowledge of the later periods of pre-history has been greatly enlarged since 1945, but the information still leaves much to be desired. Altogether, the importance of the subject is not yet matched by the quality of the available evidence.

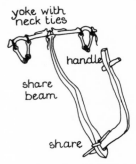

Iron-Age plough, based on the Donnerupland ard

Thus Bronze Age settlers of Surrey are only known to us as builders of barrows on Wimbledon Common and at several places on the Downs and the Lower Greensand hills, such as Godstone, Reigate, Oxted and Puttenham. The Iron Age habitation is a little clearer. The most characteristic monuments are the 'camps'. Some of these have feeble ramparts and were doubtless largely stock compounds. More spectacular are the hill-forts of the late Iron Age when defences were raised against invaders from Northern France. There is an important group of promontory and other hill and plateau forts still conspicuous along the range of Lower Greensand hills at Hascombe, Holmbury and Anstiebury. Dry Hill, Lingfield, deeper into the Weald, has an enclosure of 24 acres and a circumference of nearly a mile. The 'camps' at Farnham and Wimbledon and the ill-fated one at St. George's Hill, Weybridge, which contains modern houses within its ramparts, are examples in the Thames valley. None of these hill-forts has been fully investigated and their precise function is still debatable. Unlike the large hill-forts of Oldbury in Kent and Cissbury, Sussex, they are too small to be reckoned as embryonic towns. They were possibly the headquarters of lordships containing many scattered farms. The Wealden forts are the first signs of a permanent, settled economy based on the forest which would have become of crucial importance by reason of its iron deposits. The remarkable pattern of Saxon land division based on Anstiebury, mentioned on p. 33, suggests a degree of continuity between prehistoric and Dark Age times.

Iron Age farms have been identified at West Clandon and Hawks Hill, Leatherhead, and an ever-increasing list now suggests that a chain

Butser ancient farm, the round house

of them covered the Downs free of Clay-with-Flints. At Leatherhead the farmstead is of the Little Woodbury type. The main dwellings would have been a large round house and the pits and post holes have been orthodoxly interpreted as grain storage pits, raised granaries and corn drying racks. Few good examples of the familiar patchworks of small, squarish 'Celtic' fields have been traced in Surrey; the system on Farthing Down, Coulsdon, not discovered until 1945, is the best known.

The explanations of the maze of pits, post-holes, ditches, banks, pottery and bones found and minutely recorded on Iron Age farm sites are being tested at the Butser Ancient Farm Research Project, just across the Surrey-Hampshire border near Petersfield, the first attempt in Britain to reconstruct an Iron Age farm and work it as it might have been in *c.* 300 B.C. The visitor to Butser Hill Country Park sees below him two thatched round-houses, small rectangular fields sown with Emmer, Spelt and Celtic beans, with other primitive species of domesticated plants. A flock of diminutive, dark-woolled Soay sheep in wattle-herded enclosures, Dexter cattle (reminiscent of the leggy Iron Age *Bos longifrons*) and pigs bred from the first cross of a wild boar and a Tamworth sow, were selected as the nearest living descendants to prehistoric domestic animals. At Butser Ancient Farm experiments are being conducted to explain the daily economy of a small Iron Age farmstead. These include studies of the yields of crops sown in fields cultivated by a light plough of prehistoric type drawn by an ox team (Plate 6).

Roman Surrey

Most of 'Surrey' during the Roman occupation was divided between the neighbouring tribal territories of the Regni, whose capital was the new town of *Noviomagus Regnensium* (Chichester) and that of the Atrebates governed from *Calleva Atrebatum* (Silchester). The most important development affecting 'Surrey' was the founding of London itself as a great centre of communication by land and sea with a large population providing an important market for food and consumer goods. We have a general picture of a well-organised villa life at Ashtead and Rapsley; of a string of London outposts such as Ewell which began as posting stages on the new roads and of important pottery and tile works, probably largely dependent upon the London market. The part of 'Surrey' nearest London probably assumed the special character of the hinterland of a major city, but we are too short of archaeological facts at present to be able to express anything positive as to this expectable development. Opportunities for further excavation

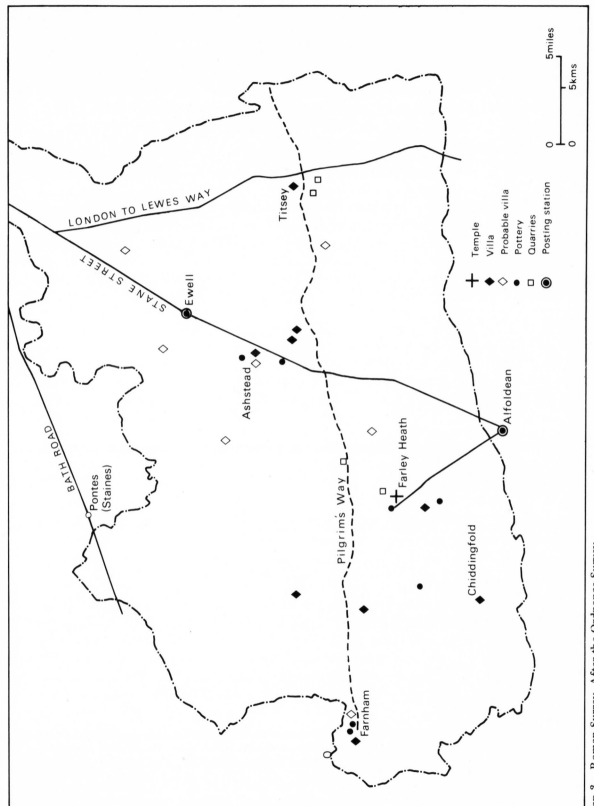

LONDON TO LEWES WAY

STANE STREET

BATH ROAD

Pontes
(Staines)

Ewell

Titsey

Ashstead

Pilgrim's Way

Farley Heath

Alfoldean

Farnham

Chiddingfold

Temple
Villa
Probable villa
Pottery
Quarries
Posting station

5miles

5kms

0

0

Map 3. Roman Surrey. After the Ordnance Survey.

are taken by archaeologists as they occur, which are unfortunately few. Gradually they are coming to grips with their intractable and ambiguous evidence. One of the most serious gaps is the lack of information about many aspects of the villas, particularly their economy and settlement patterns. In the heavily built-up parts of Surrey there are still major questions remaining (Map 3, p. 25).

Although comparatively small, the largest Roman town in 'Surrey' was the bridgehead settlement where the Roman roads of Watling Street and Stane Street converged on the south bank of the Thames to cross into Londinium. This was a sandy area divided up by streams with swamps to east and west. Excavation of bomb-damaged buildings and later investigation has revealed a Roman occupation along the riverside and a ribbon development bordering the two main roads. This urban growth appears to be of the Flavian period (69–79 A.D.). Settlement on the excavated sites is covered by dark silt layers, presumably laid down by floodwaters which mark the period of rising sea level from the early fourth century. The neglect of river embankments during the very disturbed third century in Roman Britain may have been a contributory factor in the decline of the south bank.

The villas of Surrey are not as large or as opulent as those of Kent and Sussex, but at Ashtead was a corridor-type house of at least thirteen rooms, connected to Stane Street by a flint road. Here it is archaeologically possibly to find skilled craftsmen in the late first century A.D. making box flue tiles for the villa's heating system, exquisitely impressed with the tiler's elaborate trade mark by means of patterns cut in soft stone or a wooden cylindrical die-stamping roller sheathed in bronze. At the Rapsley villa in Ewhurst was a tile factory and the Titsey villa possessed a fulling mill. The potters of the river Wey district near Farnham were noted for coarse wares. Thus Surrey early began its long history as a workshop. The recession in these industries discernible in the third century A.D. is probably related to the decline of London as a trading centre.

The Stane Street flung across the Weald is the greatest monument to the Roman practical genius in Surrey. With the aid of aerial photography and detailed fieldwork, I. D. Margary traced its entire length between Chichester and London. It is well engineered to secure the shortest route allowed by the lie of the land. Finds along the road at Dorking, Epsom, Ewell and Tooting indicate important sites of human occupation by *c.* 70 A.D. Near Ockley, Stane Street remains in use as a fine raised causeway across deep Weald clay. A splendid derelict section is traceable on a wide *agger* across Mickleham Downs between the Mole Valley and Epsom. This was carefully metalled with pebbles and flints.

Well executed 'dog and stag' relief-patterned tile die stamp, Ashtead roman villa. (after A. W. G. Lowther)

26

III Saxon Surrey

From the great political, social and religious upheaval into which the Roman province of Britannia was plunged early in the fifth century, Surrey emerged drastically changed. The name Surrey, spelt by the Venerable Bede as *Suder Ge* and in Domesday book as *Sudrie*, contains two highly significant English elements which explicitly tell us of important new events. The second syllable of the name is derived from Old English *ge,* akin to German *gau,* meaning 'inhabitants of a district or region'. The first element means 'south'. The name Surrey means therefore the 'south region'. Geographically the meaning is plain. It suggests that Surrey was originally the southern district of a Middle Saxon kingdom which included Middlesex ('Norrey') coterminous across the Thames. There is no written tradition to support this and at present no definite corroborative archaeological evidence, but it is perhaps noteworthy that the goods excavated from the early fifth century graves of Saxon federates in the Wandle valley around Croydon and Mitcham differ stylistically from those across the Medway in Kent, but resemble those found on the north and west sides of London. These graves are the earliest signs of Saxon migration into Surrey. From their location (Map 2) they appear to have been English colonies assisting the Romano-British inhabitants of London to secure the city against the flanking advance of other bands of English marauders (Map 2, p. 21).

Design of early fourteenth century floor tile

It is impossible to define precisely the area which later came to be occupied by the Saxon whose early place-names are so conspicuous in the valleys of the Wandle, Mole and Wey. The phonology of the place-names of eastern Berkshire suggests that the English people in this wooded area were of Surrey stock: for example, the people from whom Wokingham in Berkshire were named are almost certainly the same group referred to in the Surrey place-name of Woking and it is possible that the district around Sonning, and perhaps even further west around Reading, once formed part of the Surrey section of the Middle Saxon kingdom. The loss of these westerly limbs can be attributed to the successful conquests of Mercia, the Anglian kingdom of the Midlands in the seventh and eighth centuries. Reference to the One Inch Ordnance map will indicate that the county boundary of Surrey against Sussex is generally drawn in favour of the latter county. This northward penetration of Sussex at the expense of Surrey is

27

probably to be attributed to the military conquests of Aelle, the first Saxon king of Sussex, who was acknowledged as *Bretwalda,* or leader, of all the English during his lifetime.

Due to a further series of wars between neighbouring kingdoms Surrey lost not only land but its autonomy. Until 825 A.D. Surrey was politically unstable as either part of a kingdom of Mercia or of Wessex. In 666 A.D., to take a notable event by way of example, the sub-king of Surrey had to obtain the consent of King Wulfhere of Mercia before founding the Abbey of St. Peter of Chertsey. After 825 Surrey was finally annexed into the kingdom of Wessex and several of the kings of the house of Wessex were crowned at Kingston-upon-Thames.

Our knowledge of the daily life and settlement geography of Saxon Surrey during these Dark Ages, and for generations to come, turns largely upon the topographical studies drawing upon the cumulative evidence of place-names and Saxon local land charters. These enable one to trace, however shadowly, the exploitation of the land and the process by which the Saxons transformed their setting of marsh, heath and forest into farmland during the six obscure but formative centuries between the first migrations of Saxons south of the Thames in the sixth century and the making of Domesday Book in 1086. Little appreciable light on these matters is thrown by oral tradition and the contribution of archaeology is still in its infancy. Pagan cemeteries have been badly excavated on a very limited scale and findings are ill-published, whilst large-scale intensive fieldwork in the Saxon period has hardly begun.

Broadly speaking, the Saxon colonisation was from the most inviting to the most unfriendly soils for pioneer farmers. The first real English occupation of Surrey seems to have colonised all the most accessible and workable soils by the end of the fifth century. Place-names in O.E. *ham,* meaning a village community, a manor or a homestead, and O.E. *hamm,* considered to have meanings of an enclosure or a meadow by a stream, are generally reckoned to belong to an early stratum of English names. The majority of these place-names in Surrey occur north of the Pilgrim's Way in districts which have always been inviting to settlement and which were probably cleared of woodland during the Roman occupation and earlier (Map 4 p. 29).

Another indication of very early English settlement are the several place-names which were given in south-west Surrey before the coming of Christianity in the late seventh century. These heathen names include Willey, near Farnham, whose O.E. form is derived from Old English *weoh,* an idol or shrine, and *leah,* a clearing. Such religious symbols were commonly established in natural clearings in woodland. It is also suggested that the place-names of neighbouring Thursley and

Harrow from the Bayeux Tapestry

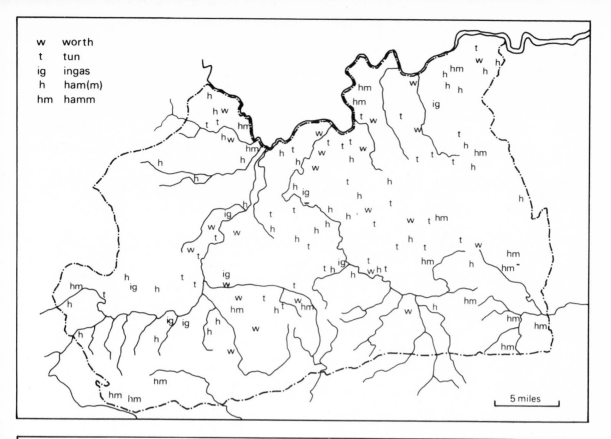

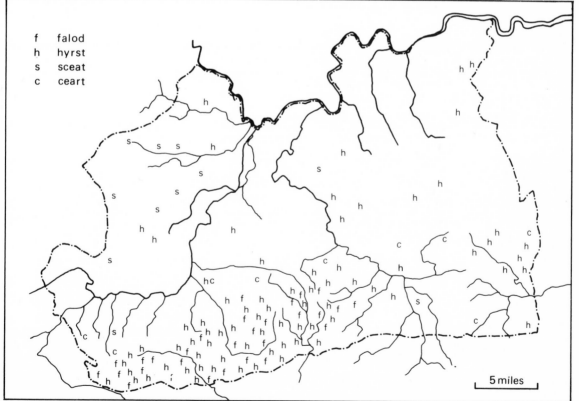

Map 4.   Saxon place-names. After J. E. B. Gover, A. Mawer and M. Stenton, *The Place-Names of Surrey*: English Place-Name Society, volume XI (1934).

Tuesley may have been clearings where the gods Thunor and Tiw were worshipped. The second element of Peper Harrow is from Old English *hearg,* a temple. Thunderfield in Horley may also indicate an open space where a shrine of Thunor was placed.

Another place-name especially interesting with regard to Surrey is Old English *ceart,* occurring only on the sands or sandstones, and surviving in the dialect of Kent and Surrey as 'chart'. It denotes 'rough, uncultivated land overgrown with gorse, broom, bracken and the like'. These 'wastes' were invariably outlying portions of manors centred on the Vale of Holmesdale.

Such place-name evidence is coarse-grained and still notoriously difficult to interpret with any degree of accuracy. It we now turn to some of the Saxon land charters we can begin to decipher the economic and social structure of some estates and their integrated nature. The King's farm or estate of Kingston-upon-Thames was sited at a ford across the river and uniquely in Surrey, its outlying, dependent farms were denoted *bartons*: Norbiton was the north *barton* and Surbiton the south *barton.* Battersea contained at least three distinct elements; the farmland at Battersea itself; the brushwood on Battersea Rise (O.E. *hris,* brushwood) and the swine pastures at Penge, a British name corresponding to the Welsh *pen* ('head') and *coed* ('wood'). In a charter of 957 A.D. we are told that the Penge woods were 'seven miles, seven furlongs and seven feet in circumference'. The Saxon riverside opposite London is full of early names. Southwark means 'the fort or defensive work of the men of Surrey'; at Walworth (Old English *Wealh,* foreigner) was the farm of the serfs of Britons, and Lambeth and Rotherhithe denote places where lambs and cattle respectively were embarked.

The most striking feature of the Saxon landscape of South-East England, however, must have been the wild and almost uninterrupted country which spread across the Wealds of Surrey, Kent and Sussex between the inward-facing North and South Downs. Over this huge tract the victory of man over an untamed nature was still to be won. The forest border long remained a natural boundary to human existence in Surrey and, although the Saxon ploughman cultivating on the edge of the great forest waste daily wore his way into it bit by bit, the forest clearance was the cumulative work of generations. It was as a swine herd and cattle-drover that the Saxon first left his mark on the forest.

The first men inhabiting the unenclosed woods or wastes in Surrey were the *drofmen,* drovers engaged in tending cattle, who, unlike other peasants, grew no corn and had no oxen for the plough. Such peasants, and also swineherds, would have divided their year between their 'winter house', their permanent abode in the village and their 'summer

Woman milking cow (medieval Ms. Bodley 764)

30

house' in the distant woodland pasture. The *drofmen* possibly took hurdles on their annual migration to the forest and by these means erected summer houses consisting only of a single room and a cattle-yard.

Saxon weaver's hut

This organisation of the inhabited space in Saxon Surrey and the long-continued custom of herding swine and cattle into the Weald for summer pasture is still reflected with remarkable clarity by the surviving road system. It is readily observable that the general direction of the close net of by-roads is from north to south. On closer examination, it will be found that each of the villages and hamlets of the Vale of Holmesdale has a direct connection with places in the deep Surrey Weald. That some of these routes, or parts of them, have become totally unnecessary is indicated by their present unmetalled condition. They seem to bring the passage of time very presently and vividly to the mind. If we now take, by way of example, the roads and trackways within the triangle bounded by Woking, Leatherhead and Horsham, many of these are traceable over quite remarkably long distances, running down from the North Downs into the heavy clays of the Weald. It is a road system which suggests that the local necessity of villagers in the Vale of Holmesdale was not so much connections between their neighbouring villages as between their village and the outlying woodland of the Weald. We are, in fact, examining the road pattern of a large number of anciently self-sufficing communities. It is a conscious design related to three main resources of each manor: the arable and meadow on the richer soils about the parent villages; the sheep pastures on Downs or heath, and the swine grazings in the Weald. This also explains the striking symmetrical distribution of rural settlement at the foot of the Chalk escarpment and along the edge of the Lower Greensand formation, for here the best soils were to be found. This gave rise to very long and narrow 'strip parishes' adapted for ecclesiastical administration. It also explains the archaic territorial characteristic of detached parishes in the Weald as outliers of parishes to the north. This complicated mosaic was remodelled by sweeping changes in the late 19th century, but on early Ordnance Survey maps the surviving fragmented pattern is observable.

The old pattern of Wealden 'outliers' can be instanced by reference to central Surrey. The scattered farmhouses of Newdigate parish are younger than its road, for the parish name probably means 'on Ewood-gate', i.e., on the road between Reigate and Rusper which passed through Ewood, a great woodland in the parish. In the earliest documents relating to Newdigate church it is designated a subordinate chapel, presumably dependent upon Reigate. Much of Burstow parish was originally part of the Archbishop of Canterbury's manor of

31

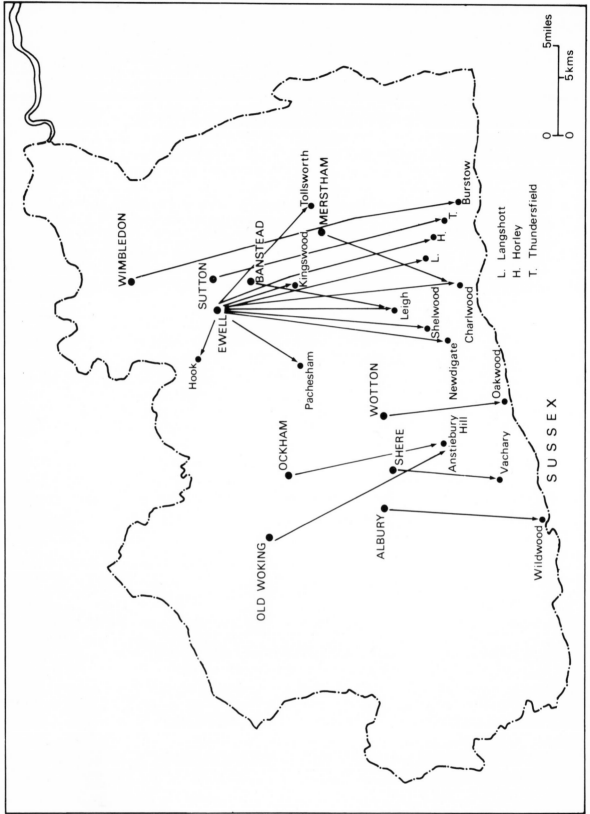

Map 5. The expansion of Saxon manors into the Weald. The *villata* of Ewell manor are based on data in Alfred Heal's *Records of Merton Priory* (1898).

Labels on map:

WIMBLEDON

SUTTON

BANSTEAD

Kingswood

Tollsworth

MERSTHAM

Burstow

L. Langshott
H. Horley
T. Thundersfield

L. H. T.

L.

EWELL

Leigh

Shelwood

Charlwood

Hook

Pachesham

WOTTON

Newdigate

Oakwood

OCKHAM

SHERE

Anstiebury Hill

Vachary

ALBURY

OLD WOKING

Wildwood

S U S S E X

0   5kms
0   5miles

5. Typical of the re-fronted houses in Surrey of the Georgian period is this fine town house at Limpsfield. The side elevation and exterior brick chimney tell of its extreme antiquity.

6. Nursecombe, a medieval hall house adapted into a yeoman's farm-house in the early 17th century.

7. (*above*) The ruins of Waverley Abbey on the banks of the River Wey.

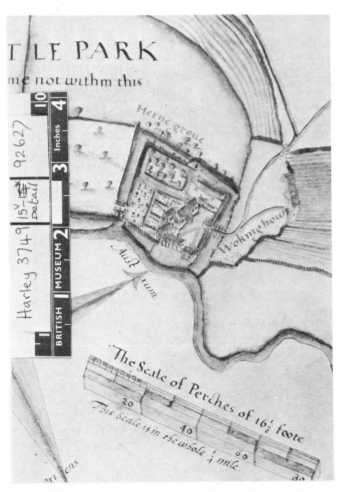

8. (*left*) Norden's plan of Old Woking (1607) clearly shows the survival of the medieval moats.

Wimbledon and Thundersfield in Horley was a swine pasture of Sutton manor. Banstead had a Wealden outlier in Leigh. When the church of Capel (Old French *Capelle,* a chapel) first appears in recorded history it is merely as a chapel-of-ease to Dorking. Oakwood was a detached part of Wotton and the status of its church has had a similar evolution to that of Capel. Much of Charlwood lay within the manor of Merstham, owned by monks of Christchurch, Canterbury. Horne was constituted as a separate parish as late as the reign of Queen Anne: until then it was a detached part of Bletchingley. Haslemere was originally dependent upon Chiddingfold, as the latter was at a more distant date to Godalming. Shere originally included Cranleigh. The men of these subordinate settlements would have been obliged originally to carry their dead for burial to the main church and to go there also to marry and to baptize their children. The steady development of chapelries into separate parishes during the later Middle Ages reflects the growing wealth and population of the Weald (Map 5, p. 32).

Woman spinning

The most remarkable parish geography in Surrey before the boundary revisions of the late 19th century was in the locality of Anstiebury Hill, a fortified camp over 800ft. above sea level in the fern and heather district of Leith Hill. The camp was surrounded within one hundred yards by no less than six parishes—Abinger, Shere, Cranleigh, Ewhurst, Ockley and Ockham (in Woking Hundred), of which the last four were detached parts of their respective parishes. Malden has argued, probably correctly, that this arrangement of parishes can hardly be fortuitous. The small size of the outlying portions appears to rule out their origin as swine pastures. It is conceivable, as Malden has suggested, that we have here a unique relict of a Saxon expedient analogous to 'castle-guard'; that is an arrangement providing for the upkeep of defences by specifically allotting land revenues for this purpose amongst the contributing communities.

The pattern of roads, place-names and ecclesiastical organisation can thus tell us a great deal about the forest economy of Saxons in Surrey. Place-names also reveal much about the chronology and course of wood clearing. Most of the place-names of the Surrey Weald are much older than the villages or farms themselves. The sites later chosen for human habitation had generally already a well-known name as long-used pastures in summer or as hunting grounds. Thus the name Oxted means 'place of oak trees'; Pyrford 'the ford marked by pear trees'; Horsley (East and West) 'the horses' clearing'; Nutfield 'open space with nut trees or hazels'; Reigate 'open space where the roe-deer were hunted'; Limpsfield 'open space amidst the elms'.

As human habitations many of these pastures, as we have seen,

33

*Swine slaughtering
(Corpus Christi Coll.)*

evolved from a stage of temporarily occupied huts or shelters associated with seasonal pastoral farming before they were permanently inhabited by farmers who cultivated land within ring-fenced fields. This evolution is one of the most characteristic of the Surrey Weald. The evidence for the change from one stage to the next is less than for successive stages of settlement. Very characteristic of the west Surrey low Weald and the adjoining part of Sussex are the sites of large farmhouses and of Saxon and early Norman churches bearing the suffix *-fold* (O.E. *falod*). These *folds* are invariably found on the low swells of better-drained soil of a lighter texture and brown colour. They help to recall the ancient forest landscape and the earliest graziers because the word denotes staking off as pasture ground for a cattle (or swine) pen into which the animals would have been herded at night. The very general use of the suffix suggests that the Wealdsmen who pitched their *folds* in the openings within the woods were originally herders of animals rather than farmers. The *fold* was therefore the germ of a farm and, later still, often a village. The original dwelling, probably surrounded by a cleared space of only a few acres, was built on the border of the drove road or wood path which ultimately grew into a village street.

When the *folds* and also *dens* and *shots* (derived from O.E. *den* and *scydd*, meaning woodland pastures, especially for swine) passed into permanent occupation is one of the unresolved puzzles of Surrey history. We cannot answer the question with any assurance for whereas, for most parts of England, Domesday provides some idea of the extent of the clearings at the end of the eleventh century, the Surrey folios are not an adequate source of settlement history for they do not separately enumerate colonists in the outlying Wealden parts of manors based on its northern periphery. Yet circumstantial evidence that agriculture and settlement had made considerable headway in the Weald is impressive. Of special importance is the evidence that churches had been founded in Wealden parishes to serve the scattered community growing there. This evidence reinforces Lennard's injunction that 'we must not be too ready to fill the vacant spaces of the Domesday map with imagined woodland or marsh'. His conclusion that places with large numbers of peasants assigned to them in the Surrey Domesday incorporate population in unmentioned places in the outlying Weald is almost certainly correct.

There is thus every reason to believe that the stature of the Saxon achievement in clearing and colonising the Surrey Weald has been greatly under-estimated. The sharp crack of the axe must have repeatedly rung out through the woodland as every year the sown land gained on the wild. The ring of the axe strokes denoted farmers making rough huts and fencing them off before clearing their first fields.

34

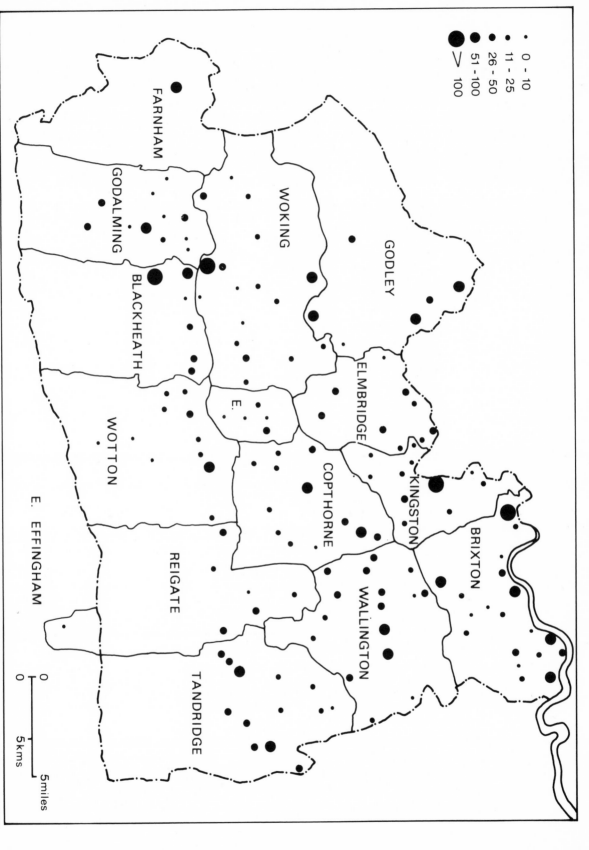

Map 6. Recorded population in the Domesday Survey. Based on the data provided by John Morris in *Domesday Book: Surrey* (Phillimore 1976). The largest symbols need to be spread out, as it were, by eye over the surrounding blank areas. The manors are grouped into the old administra-

Legend:
- 0 - 10
- 11 - 25
- 26 - 50
- 51 - 100
- 100

FARNHAM

GODALMING

WOKING

GODLEY

BLACKHEATH

ELMBRIDGE

E.

WOTTON

COPTHORNE

KINGSTON

BRIXTON

REIGATE

WALLINGTON

TANDRIDGE

E. EFFINGHAM

0   5 miles

0   5 kms

Rich persons portrayed in an eleventh century manuscript

For many generations farming doubtless partook of the character of pioneering, but the land slowly responded to human effort. By centuries of succeeding labour the rank clays were gradually rendered fertile, each generation adding a little to the family stock. By Domesday, most of the Weald land had been fully colonised, though population was doubtless very sparse. Settlements with names ending in -ley (*leah*) are definitely the result of Saxon woodland clearance. Eleven such settlements are recorded in Domesday. Bletchingley, Witley, Henley in Ash and the two Horsleys, East and West, had become extensive clearings and the nuclei of substantial manors. The others are relatively small openings in the woods inhabited by a small cluster of peasant farms.

A world apart from the raw Weald of Saxon times were the embryonic towns. Eashing, now a mere village, was a failure; Guildford in the superior position at a convenient crossing of the river Wey superseding it. Eashing is mentioned in the *Burghal Hidage* of *c.* 900–924 as one of the defended towns spaced approximately 25–30 miles apart which the inhabitants of the kingdom of Wessex were to use as refuges against the Danes. The leading Saxon town, as in Roman times, was Southwark, also first mentioned in the *Burghal Hidage* as *Suthringa geweorcke*, 'the defensive work of the men of Surrey'. By the 11th century, Southwark had grown into a large town. The intimate connection between many Surrey villages and the essential life of London in the 11th century is indicated by dwellings in London and Southwark appurtenant to rural manors. In Domesday these properties are confined to manors south and south-west of London. Not only were nearer manors such as Lambeth, Bermondsey, Mortlake, Merton and Long Ditton in possession of property in the City of London, but so also were more distant manors such as Bletchingley, Godstone (Walkingstead), Banstead and Walton-on-the-Hill. The correspondence between this distribution and the map of Dark Age pagan burial sites (p. 21) is so close that it is difficult not to believe that the latter is an explanation. Another link between London and Surrey was corn-milling. At Battersea the activity accounted for half the value of the manor. The Domesday data of population (Map 6, p. 35) suggests a scantily peopled countryside.

Plough from the Bayeux Tapestry

IV Medieval Farming and Woodmanship

Much of Surrey in the middle ages was not a very promising environment for commercial agriculture. The Weald was one of these areas. The intractability of its cold, thin clay soils became a by-word, and, in addition, soils were deficient in phosphate, calcium, potassium and nitrogen. Fields could not be worked upon without some preliminary improvement to the soil and they could not stand up to wet spells. In a hot dry summer, the soil dried up like a brick, making it impossible to prepare the ground for sowing. Agriculture was a matter of considerable expense and difficulty and, on account of the miry roads, large areas were scarcely accessible for much of the year. Few cultivated parts of England yielded a less ready and reliable return to the man who drove the plough. Cultivated fields quickly became foul and exhausted and required periods of rest, except on specially treated ground. Medieval cropping was on a basis of convertible (alternate) husbandry under which system a relatively small proportion of the arable was cultivated on a quasi-permanent basis with the aid of generous manuring. The remaining fields underwent short bouts of continuous cultivation and then rested for a similar period to recuperate.

Unquestionably, the principal manure used for land improvement was marl. A direct application of lime from the nearest source along the distant Chalk rim of the Weald became practicable only with the more abundant horses and wagons of the 17th century. The medieval farmer, accustomed to dear carriage and cheap labour, made the marl pit do the duty of a lime kiln. A pit was dug in the corner of almost every field and farmers winched up calcareous clay found in subordinate beds below the top-soil and spread it over each field before ploughing about once in 20 years. Almost every part of the Surrey Weald bears witness to this extraordinary exertion.

Nearly all the Wealdsman raised he consumed at home. Probably only his annual crop of calves broke out of the circle of subsistence for beasts were marketable on the hoof. He worked his small farm with the aid of his family and farms to this day often bear the names of their 13th- or 14th-century occupiers. He judged the value of land by the number of cows it kept and woodland by the size of the herd of swine it fattened. Each little community of farmers had its own artisans such as weavers, carpenters, smiths and potters, which supplied it with its local needs. Apart from periodic visits to the nearest market

Monumental brasses of Robert Skern and his wife, Kingston-upon-Thames, 1437

37

Medieval tithe barn

town and occasional errands to London on the lord's business, their life was spent within very narrow bounds.

In the 13th century when population was growing at an unprecedented speed new land was called for year after year. There was a considerably higher labour and capital input applied to the Surrey Weald than at any previous period and not matched until the hey-day of the iron industry three centuries later. This greatly extended the limits of cultivation at the expense of woodland. The field-name *ruding* or *riding* (derived from Old English [*ge*]*ryd*, to grub up trees) frequently met with, is usually one of these late clearings. With the help of these names we can see the Weald in its youth, undergoing an early stage in its process of self-development, which has continued to the present.

An important aspect of man's husbandry in the clearings was its effect on the evolution of rural settlement. The single farms carved out of the waste in the early middle ages were progressively improved by each succeeding generation. Many original holdings eventually reached a stage of human development when they could support several families who also took in additional land to make the new holdings more viable. Many single farms had evolved by the early 14th century in this way into a loose hamlet cluster or 'globule'. From the 18th century, when a rural exodus to the towns began, the little holdings were invariably amalgamated to make more arable on each remaining farming unit. Accordingly, there was frequently a devolution from the 'globule' settlement to a large farm. The still remaining farmhouses, no longer housing farmers, are the clues to this process in the present landscape.

Another developing district was the Royal Forest of Windsor, formerly a wild tract of country nine miles wide, and extending across 17 parishes in north-west Surrey and the adjoining part of Berkshire. Forest used in this sense was neither a botanical nor a geographical term, but a legal one. The word is derived from the Latin *foris,* meaning outside, and was applied to land where the Common Law of England did not pertain. The territory 'afforested' in the case of the Forest of Windsor was largely heathland developed on the sterile sands of the Bagshot Sands formation. A document of considerable topographical interest is the Forest Regarder's rent roll of 1372. It begins by detailing the specific landmarks along the boundary of the Forest which has been identified in a recent perambulation. These are of particular interest, because the perambulation is one of the earliest authentic descriptions of the Surrey landscape that we possess. The bounds can be followed on the One Inch sheets of the Ordnance Survey maps and also on John Norden's beautiful (but very inaccurate) map of the Forest made in 1607 (Plate 18).

38

Although the progressive clearing of woodland in the early middle ages was the main process of landmaking in Surrey, the reclamation of the heathland in the Forest of Windsor was also an important process in the development of its peasant society. There were many surviving areas of opportunity for the colonist. In the late 13th century the Crown empowered its Constable of Windsor to enclose and lease out for cultivation all the old sheepwalks near villages within the Forest and peasants secured the right to fence meadow and fields with a growing hedge in these parts of the Forest. The Abbots of Chertsey and Westminster conferred similar facilities. Slowly the sown land gained at the expense of the wild. At Pyrford the Abbot of Westminster had between 160-170 tenants in 1330, 70 of them cottagers or smallholders, and the swelling rent roll suggests that the village was growing right up to the Black Death. On the Abbey of Chertsey's estate Chobham and other vills were growing at the same period. Within the bounds of the Royal Forest itself Chobham, Frimley, Horsell, Ottershaw, Pirbright, Pyrford and Worplesdon were also filling up with small peasants. Most of the cottagers cultivated their tiny plots more like kitchen gardens than farms, sowing a little winter and summer corn in regular succession without respite. It is unlikely that the soil could have borne good crops for more than a few years at a time with the little manure available. The many Forest grants of virgin soil held by the same tenants may therefore reflect this need for fresh land.

One of these little peasant farmers is immortalised in the records of the Abbey of Chertsey. When his holding was confiscated by the Abbot because he was farming it badly in 1332, William de Brok of Chobham owned four oxen, seven steers, two cows, 2½ quarters of winter wheat and 5 quarters of oats—just enough perhaps to feed a family on good white bread and to earn a little money in the market place. As his holding could not support all his livestock, William de Brok would have run his animals on the common and also cut fern for litter, later to be applied as manure to his meadows. He would also have prepared his pork by smoke strongly impregnated with the pungent aroma of burning peat, also produced by the Forest, and his evening light was probably simply a rush dipped in grease. In every way William de Brok is a forerunner of the race of 'broom-squires' who re-peopled the wastes in the 18th and 19th centuries.

Pier caps, c. 1200, Old Court Cottage, Limpsfield (after R. T. Mason)

Although the frequent grants and encroachments made before 1350 gradually lessened the area of the Forest it still held out for the most part, and after the Black Death, when the demand for land slackened, many of the holdings reverted to waste.

One way of tracing the most anciently farmed Surrey countryside is by examining the evidence afforded by the hedgerows themselves. Dr. Max Hooper has suggested that there may be a correlation between the age of a hedge and a number of different shrub species growing in it. The count of the shrubs (as defined in a standard list and along a 30-yard stretch of hedge) gives the approximate age of the hedge in centuries. A 19th-century Enclosure Act hedge will typically have only one or two species; a hedge planted by a Tudor or Stuart 'improver' can be expected to have four or five species, whilst a hedge which has 10 or more shrubs in 30 yards could well be of Saxon origin. The reasons underlying this relation between age and the number of shrub species are complex and little understood, and readers are referred to the work of Pollard, Hooper and Moore (1974). Despite the destruction of old hedgerows in Surrey for the sake of larger fields, many fine old examples of hedgerow still survive. The very old hedges were commonly planted on a wide earthbank bordered by a ditch acting as a deep water run to carry water off upland fields in wet seasons. In this habitat elderberry, field maple, dog rose, hawthorn, hazel, sloe and bullace thrive, interlaced with honeysuckle and trailing brambles or woody plants such as traveller's joy and clematis.

It is too early to judge whether Hooper's hypothesis is applicable to Surrey. Sample tests suggest that some hedge counts are correlated with age. The hedges bordering Roundals Lane, Hambledon (the old road to Petworth), for example, average about eight to nine species which could give them an origin about 1000 A.D., which is quite acceptable in the light of the general documentary evidence. Again, the species growing on a fine hedge near Shoelands, Puttenham, which is in older settled country, number up to 11 species, but this has been managed until recently to produce a full range of timber for local wood workers (principally oak, ash and hazel). Many other Surrey hedges have been similarly planted up for the timber trade and on large estates game shelters and ornament explain the riotous and abundant hedgerows, supporting up to 14 and, exceptionally, 16 'countable' species. Around Haslemere there are many of this type.

The wood-clearing techniques of pioneer farmers have also contributed to the present landscape in another way. Unlike other districts enclosed directly from the wild, many fields were not bounded by narrow, crooked hedgerows, but by strips of woodland up to 33ft. wide, locally known as shaws or *rewes*. Such shaws certainly formed part of the medieval landscape for field-names incorporating this element are recorded from the 13th century. William Marshall attributed this local custom to the exceptionally large nursery of oak, ash, hedge-maple and hazel trees needed by Wealden farmers who supplied markets in fuel (including charcoal for the iron

Medieval tree-pruner (Ms. Corpus Christi Coll. 285)

40

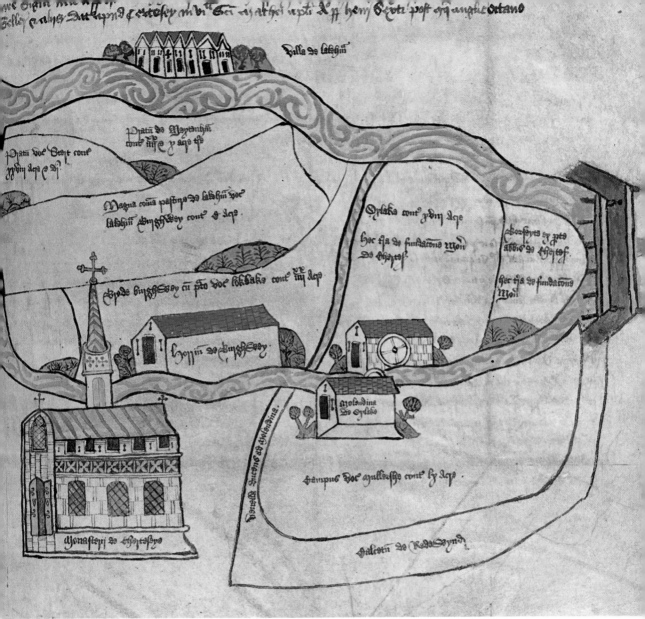

9. A late 15th century plan of Chertsey Abbey and its demesnes. The village of Laleham is depicted at the top; the Abbey is shown at the bottom. The barn on Burgheye, built by Abbot John Rutherwyk in 1315 is shown, together with mills, a fish weir, a large common pasture belonging to Laleham and several fields.

10. Cider making, an important Surrey institution in the middle ages.

11. Hambledon church, typical of the unpretentious little churches in sparsely populated parishes before the heavy-handed 'restoration' and re-building of the Victorians.

12. Crossways Farm, Abinger, a good example of a brick fronted small house of the early 17th century, the home of a wool merchant.

13. William Schellinck's *Epsom Common and Wells*, 1662. The scene shown was ¾ mile west of Epsom village. A small building houses the Wells and people can be seen taking the waters behind the railings. Note the horse-riding, the chief recreation.

14. J. Esselens' view of Kingston-upon-Thames from Coombe Hill, *c.*1650. The Surrey Hills are in the distance. Hampton Court Palace is shown on the extreme right.

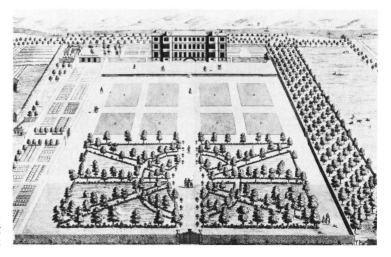

15. These formal gardens of 17th century Ham House are now being restored by the National Trust

16. 18th century prospect of Richmond.

17. The Terrace and the view from Richmond Hill by Leonard Knyff (1650-1722).

industry) and shipbuilding timber. Moreover, in a region where soil was mediocre and land cheap and plentiful, the shaw provided a fence with a mimimum of effort and expense. The little fields of the pioneer farmer—typically only two-four acres in size—gave hardly room for the plough and were often too cold and poor to be ploughed with profit. They were, however, considered by early farmers as ideal for livestock, affording good shelter and a series of 'paddocks' for use in rotation. This 'old way of very small fields for the stock' persisted into the mid-19th century when under-draining led to the grubbing up of many hedgerows, and destruction since has been very considerable. Yet fossilised medieval fields still exist in fragmentary patchworks. Not all shaws are of medieval origin; many are evidently of later plantings. It was complained of a 16th-century Camberwell farmer that he had permitted his hedgerow to grow beyond the statutory width of 4ft. 6ins. prescribed in the manorial regulations.

Threshing (Corpus Christi Coll.)

In the 13th and 14th centuries the valuation placed for fiscal purposes upon land of a deceased major landowner (contained in *Inquisitiones post mortem*) provides illuminating information as to the use of land in Surrey at this period. Used with caution, they show how practically-minded farmers responded to their environmental burdens or opportunities. The maximum efficiency of agriculture of most of medieval England was probably reached under a three-course rotation of wheat, barley or oats, and fallow, thus leaving one-third of the farmland almost idle in any given year. In some specially favoured districts such as the coastlands of Norfolk, north Kent and coastal Sussex, fallowing was reduced and corn yields were probably higher. Sheep stocks in these coastal districts were large. It is significant that much of Surrey failed to reach even the intensity of land use based on the standard three-course. In the Weald, arable farming was greatly extended during the 13th century, but it sharply contracted following the severe reduction in population as a result of the Black Death of 1348–9 and much land presumably lapsed back to woodland and scrub for want of a market. On the lean sandy soils of the Lower Greensand formation, only a half of the field acreage, or even less, was apparently cultivated at any one time. The proportion of arable rose on Downland soils, but it was of low value because of its dry, hilly and stony nature. It is only near London, on the richer soils of the Thames valley, and also in the Vale of Holmesdale below the Chalk escarpment in the middle of the county that manors achieved something like a two-thirds use of arable land. One or two estates will be singled out for special mention. Wotton, near Dorking, is again considered in some detail in Chapter IX. The surviving *Inquisitiones* record an intensity of land use ranging from a 'low' of only 40 arable

41

*Interior, Newdigate
Church (after Harper,
The Brighton Road)*

acres out of 200 in 1300 to a 'high' of 80 acres in 1282. This estate
straddled the Vale of Holmesdale, but included much rough Chalkland
and sandy heath. It can probably be regarded as a microcosm of Surrey.
Since there is no evidence that the crop yields of the peasantry differed
to any extent from those of the larger landowners we must assume a
lower level of agricultural production in Surrey than from its neighbouring counties. The royal administration seems to have taken this
into account for when the sheriffs were required to provision the king's
armies abroad the sheriff of Surrey's burden was smaller than would
have been warranted on the basis of the county's acreage alone.

In the Weald most of the farmland was probably taken into separate
occupation from the very first clearance of the wood. A Wealden
farmer's lot was a hard one, but he was his own master: the handles
of his own plough made him feel free. The lord's demesne in the
Weald, and generally in Surrey, was consolidated into separate parcels
and farmed separately. The peasants' land outside the Weald was apparently dispersed in common fields, but its enclosure into small hedged
fields had begun by the early 15th century and when the earliest
estate maps become available in the late 16th and early 17th centuries
only fragmentary common field systems survived in Surrey. The reason
for the early enclosure was probably the necessity for a flexible farming
system on soils equally suitable for arable and pasture. Common fields
survived longest where the soils were light enough for sheep folding,
the cheapest and most effective way of manuring arable strips.

If Surrey was a place of medieval abundance, it was in its store of
fruit and forest trees. Regarding fruit and gardening, the art of
horticulture and fruit-growing had by the 14th century already made
Surrey a land of gardens. In the Weald fruit-growing was practised
(for subsistence purposes) on a considerable scale. For want of good
barley (an unsuitable crop on the heavy soils), an orchard for cider
and apple-butter was early planted on every farm. Elsewhere in Surrey
the 'great gardens' attached to manor houses were remarkably well
stocked with fruit trees, and the dry, stony soils of the Chalk were
plentifully furnished with vineyards. Throughout medieval Surrey,
but particularly in the middle and south, cider-drinking was a great
institution. All the manor farms belonging to Merton College, Oxford,
possessed a cider-press, and cider-making was one of the great festivals
of the farming year (Plate 10).

The rapidly-expanding English economy of the 13th and early 14th
centuries greatly increased the demand for timber and fuel. This led
to a changing attitude about the remaining Surrey woodland. Men
became studious less to cut down trees than to plant them. It became

Medieval church chest an increasingly precious resource which needed conservation. The

42

Church and the great estates set an example. Good John Rutherwyke, Abbot of Chertsey from 1307 to 1346 (whose unflagging zeal and prudence in estate management must have been hard to rival) sowed acorns and planted young oaks in his hedgerows and groves, doubtless to supplement woods that had been too heavily exploited. Great timber beams from the Abbey's estate can still be seen in the fine churches of Great Bookham and Egham, the finest monuments remaining in the present landscape of this great abbot. We can also trace attempts to protect and tend trees as crops in the form of enclosed coppices for firewood, charcoal, hurdles, fencing, etc. This involved the regular felling near the ground level of hazel, alder and other broad-leaved species which reproduced from fresh shoots from the stump (or stool). By the early 13th century in Surrey, and probably from a much earlier period, the principle of cutting this underwood on rotation of six to 12 years was widely practised.

At Farleigh near Croydon another thread of woodmanship can be unravelled. This was the practice of growing standards (mature oak and beech trees) above the lower storey of coppice. This was the traditional Surrey system of tree-growing to meet the demands of firewood and charcoal for London and also of timber for shipbuilding and building construction. Farleigh was an estate of Merton College, Oxford, and from its documents its officials are shown to be very attentive to efficient woodland management in the 14th and 15th centuries, not basically different from principles practised today. The prime object of the coppice-with-standards system is to ensure a constant supply of well-developed standard trees of different ages in the same wood, so as to produce the highest possible sustained yield of suitable timber. By 1487 the College officials were specifying the number of standards which were to be left at each cutting and stipulating the kind of cattle-proof fence which was to be erected around the cut-over ground. The actual words of a deed of sale make this plain. The College required that all the old *stathelles* (the dialect form of standards) growing in a coppice 'left standing at the last felling and before' were to be uncut and also that new standards 'most able to bear the wind' were to be additionally left on each acre. The woodmen were also required to make a good sound hedge around the cut wood and to make 'two new skletyng gates of heart of oak, well hanged easily with hook and eyetells of iron . . .'. Here we have a rare glimpse of medieval craftsmen at work. The woods enhanced the Surrey landscape near the Selsdon hotel where one can 'still walk in the high woods and smell the Surrey air'. It was the well-managed forestry on such English estates that influenced the later Tudor legislation helping to make good forestry in the realm more universal.

Medieval sower. (Corpus Christi Coll.)

43

V Churches and Religious Houses

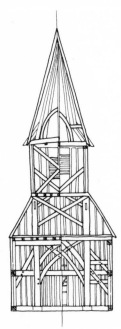

Fifteenth century wooden tower and spire, St. Peter's Church, Newdigate (after Surrey Vernacular Architecture Group)

Surrey churches are distinguished by the amount of wood used in their construction, appropriately for a county full of good timber but lacking in good stone and thinly inhabited by people in the past. Only Essex has a greater heritage of timber churches. The skill of the medieval carpenter is abundantly evident in the elaborate timber bell-towers or turrets constructed in the 14th and 15th centuries. The Wealden churches of Burstow, Horley, Horne, Leigh and Newdigate were all provided with ingenious timber towers in this period. At Leigh and Horne, the medieval tower has been replaced by a later structure. The timber tower of Burstow is a splendid piece of medieval carpentry, largely unrestored, retaining massive beams and posts hewn from locally-grown oak. Burstow still retains some of its former aspect as a woodland clearing before the Norman Conquest. One can enjoy in the churchyard the cool shade of broad-foliaged trees that melt gradually into woodland, like a garden into a wilderness. Unfortunately, the beautifully warm local sandstone of the church interior was plastered over in the heavy-handed 'restoration' of the church in 1882. A framed water colour by A. A. Sykes placed in the church discloses its former beauty. When this modern plaster is scraped off, Burstow will again be a fine specimen of a simple Wealden church. The tower of Horley is of similar construction and date, possibly built by the same craftsmen as that of Burstow. Newdigate's massive double-braced corner posts support brilliantly contrived timber-work, though rather over-restored. Thursley, formerly a chapel-of-ease of Witley, is famous for its lofty octagonal wooden steeple which has risen on four unusual corner posts from the centre of the nave since the 15th century. Hascombe and Hambledon churches also possessed a wooden steeple in this position. Tandridge has a bell turret with a shingled spire on the west gable and smaller timber belfries still exist at Alfold, Bisley, Byfleet, Crowhurst, Dunsfold, Esher, Elstead, Thames Ditton and Warlingham, amongst others (Plate 11).

Surrey churches are also distinguished by their wooden screens. Compton church possesses the oldest such screen in England, a Norman example. Many other beautiful medieval screens still survive, as at Gatton, West Horsley, Leatherhead, Nutley, Reigate and Shere, but none of these can rival the exquisite craftsmanship of the cornice of the screen at Charlwood. In smaller and poorer churches, a single

44

timber and plaster screen served as a division between nave and chancel. Chelsham and Warlingham churches both possessed such a division and one is still finely preserved in Elstead church.

Waverley Abbey holds a position of great importance in English history as the first house of the reformed order of Benedictines, called Cistercians from their head house at Cîteaux in Burgundy. This precedence was due to the encouragement of Walter Giffard, Bishop of Winchester, whose original endowment of land in his manor of Farnham enabled 13 monks from Aûmone in Normandy to found Waverley in 1128. These monks proved to be of commanding energy, resource and dedication, and exerted great influence on the general life of the English nation. Several of them became abbots of later Cistercian foundations. Eventually 128 Cistercian houses were founded in England, and Waverley, as the first of these, was recognised as the premier abbey of the order in this country.

The Cistercians practised the strict rule of not building houses in cities, castles or villages, and devoted their lives to meditation and scholarship. Waverley Abbey was beautifully sited on the banks of the river Wey two miles south of Farnham, on a sandy waste. This site was subject to recurrent floods in the 13th and early 14th centuries which damaged the conventual buildings and caused great hardship. The great monastic church, one of the largest and most splendid in the country, was moulded by the religious and architectural ideals of the high middle ages, a most creative epoch. This church has since been almost completely destroyed but it is not difficult to see it in imagination because the still existing ruin at Fountains in Yorkshire was very similar in scale and design. The conventual buildings when fully laid out embodied the principles of church planning in the 12th century. The precincts of the abbey were enclosed by walls and entered by several gateways giving access to various monastic buildings— infirmary, dormitory, lodgings at the abbot, guest house, refectory, brewhouse and stables—and all that was necessary for the self-contained life of the monks. These buildings were grouped about cloisters giving access to all the apartments and were the resort of the brethren during the hours set apart for meditation and study. This knowledge of the plan of Waverley is due to archaeological excavation, for the post-Reformation history of the abbey is one of centuries of neglect and ill-usage and little now survives above ground. Most of the building stone was robbed for fine new houses. Even since Aubrey's visit at the end of the 17th century the ruins have become much less extensive: 'Within the walls of the abbey were sixty acres . . . here also remain walls of a fair church, the walls of the cloisters and some part of the cloisters themselves . . . here was also a handsome chapel larger than

Detail of medieval wall painting (St. Margaret) Charlwood Church

45

Waverley Abbey

that of Trinity College in Oxford . . . the Hall was very spacious and noble . . .' Bestowed on Waverley were numerous endowments of land, much of it virgin wasteland, some of which the monks reclaimed and which became the economic basis of the monks' life. Distant properties were exploited as sub-stations called granges at, for example, Leigh, Tongham, Neaham, near Alton, and Wanborough. Despite the magnificence of its church, its properties were not highly valued, and in 1536, when the annual value of Waverley was assessed at under £200, it was suppressed by Thomas Cromwell as one of the lesser monasteries (Plate 7).

Rural solitude and green closes are not always spurs and incentives. In great contrast to Waverley's environment and outlook was the Cluniac abbey of Bermondsey, founded in 1082, on the very edge of the daily hubbub of London. This house owed its existence to a marked religious revival in England following the Norman Conquest when the country was again closely in touch with the church on the continent. Bermondsey was made subject to the house of St. Mary's at Charité-sur-Loire whose monks founded it. Bermondsey's first patron was Alwin Child, a citizen of London, and its benefactors included many other merchants, as well as royalty. Bermondsey's location tended to draw it into the mainstream of national life: for example, a custom sprang up of bestowing sanctuary on important royal and other individuals on the prerogative of the Crown and the great size of the monastery and its convenient location made it the venue for large church assemblies and councils of state. Not surprisingly, Bermondsey acquired vast landed possessions in Surrey and Kent and other lands and rents scattered over England.

The Abbey of St. Peter of Chertsey was a Benedictine foundation of 666 A.D. which had the distinction of being the oldest religious house in Surrey. It suffered terrible devastation at the hands of the Danes in the late 9th century, when the abbot and all his monks were slaughtered. The house was re-colonised from Abingdon and a new church was raised. It then became one of the largest and most influential of English monasteries. The Abbey's records are fullest for the first half of the 14th century when they exemplify the administrative ability of Abbot John de Rutherwyke (1307-1346) which has already been noted. The Abbey's role as a vigorous coloniser of the sandy heaths bordering the Forest of Windsor is also very significant. The efficient administration of this great house in the 15th century is evidenced by the unique survival of a map of its demesnes land, the earliest known in England (Plate 9).

VI Living in Medieval Town and Countryside

With the aid of surviving surveys and detailed room inventories we can, as it were, tour some of the 14th-century Surrey manor houses, vicariously stepping from room to room, and savour some of the old atmosphere of medieval buildings. Old Woking manor house on a branch of the river Wey, was one of the grandest. Here in 1327 was a great hall, a private chapel for its owners and another for the household, two chambers with a pantry and buttery adjoining, a kitchen, bakehouse, brewhouse, fulling house and laundry. Under another roof were three apartments for the Knight's treasurer and chief officer, and two further apartments for visiting knights and esquires. This complex of buildings was surrounded by moats (Plate 10). On the far side of the outer moat was a guardhouse with apartments. The orchard was enclosed within another moat and a second drawbridge and gate led into it. On the outside of the second moat were farm-buildings—stalls, barton (the main barn), two granges, rickyards, stables, cartsheds, ox-stall, cowshed and sheepcote. To keep the moats plentifully supplied with water, a water-wheel baled water from a reservoir. The moats at Old Woking have since been drained, but the quiet old village street with its fine houses and mellow Surrey brick retains much of the atmosphere of the past (Plate 8).

Medieval household furniture (after Gertrude Jekyll)

Thorncroft in Leatherhead was a lesser manor house of Merton College, Oxford. A detailed inventory exists of the furniture and goods in each of its rooms in April 1346, when it was let for the use of a bailiff, which accounts for the spartan furnishing. In the hall we would have found a central table with four trestles, side tables and two little forms, dishes, platters, goblets, etc. In a corner stood the wine press ready for the next season's grapes from the vineyard. This room was evidently the place where the farm servants ate their meals. On the well-scrubbed ashen tables in the dairy was the cheese-making equipment which produced cheeses for sale in the London markets. The solar contained only one long bench. In the store-room were kept the usual tools of agriculture, such as cart-wheels, forks, harrows, spades, ropes, ladders and the cider-press. When William Blakelode (who took over the reeve-ship of Thorncroft from Old William, his father) yoked his plough team, two horses led his six oxen, a rather quicker form of traction than the pondering gait of the standard eight-oxen team. The College's livestock that became his responsibility

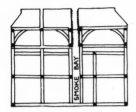

Brittleware, Charlwood, a four bay central smoke-bay house (after Surrey Vernacular Architecture Group)

included three carthorses, five riding horses, 14 oxen, 11 cows, and 250 sheep. Clearly it was not one of the larger Surrey farms.

Numerous medieval hall houses have survived in Surrey, many of them in the Weald. In the single parish of Charlwood, 28 such houses, built before 1550, have been discovered. These include nine little cottages originally with a hall of two bays open to the roof, or with one end roofed over and reached by a ladder, and 12 large hall houses, well built of good quality materials and embellished with the refinements of carvings and mouldings. These latter would have been the homes of well-to-do farmers. The best end, with the solar bedroom, was furthest away from the service end and the entrance. The room under the solar was used as a parlour or as a second bedroom, or as a store. Most medieval houses were entered immediately into the hall. Some large houses had wings, probably part of the original house. Highworth Farm has survived with remarkable little alteration. The dairy is an outshot added to the cool north-east corner. The stone floor still exists here, but it has been removed from the hall since the late 19th century. The house frame was filled in split oak and the wattle was of hazel twigs.

A prominent feature of the Wealden landscape was the moated homestead. Almost each parish has vestiges of several moated sites, still imperfectly surveyed and gazetteered. In Burstow an unusually large number are recorded. There are six definite sites (Old Lodge, Burstow Lodge, Rede Hall, Crullings, Cognans Farm, and a site in the grounds of the present Rectory) and two further possible sites—Burstow Park and Dowlands Farm. Three sites have been noted in the parish of Horley and three sites are known in Horne. Distribution tends to bear out the thesis that moated sites were manor houses, but 'the relation between topography and manorial records is at best only tenuously understood', writes one recent worker. The moated site in the Rectory grounds at Burstow is the only Surrey site to be excavated. It yielded pottery tentatively dated to the 14th century and other archaeological evidence suggested that it had been occupied from the late 13th down to the end of the 14th century. Unfortunately, deep garden-raking had destroyed almost all traces of the building that stood on the site. The location and small size of the moat suggests that it was the site of an earlier Rectory. Apart from this hardly any scientific excavation has been done to record the unseen structure of moated sites.

A detailed account of expenses incurred in the rebuilding in 1497 by Merton College of its manor-house at Thorncroft throws much light on building operations of the time and it is also an important historical record of architectural change. Twelve loads of hewn timber were

Medieval kitchen utensils

48

sent from Newdigate and seven from Leigh, both in the Weald, and a further 16 from Chessington: these places were neighbouring properties of the College. An extra payment was made to the Chessington carters whose loads had stuck fast in the mire, and supplies from Newdigate took two days to cover the six miles to Leatherhead for the same reason. From Leigh, Ockley and Little Bookham came six oak trees, each as gifts to the Warden and Fellows. Forty loads of flint stones and 7,000 tiles were amongst other building materials used. The building work included the construction of two 'chimnenes'; the lofting over of the hall to provide a set of rooms on the upper floor; and also an 'outlay', i.e., a wing at ground level. Salt was procured for the hearth, presumably as a lining to prevent soot adhering to the sides of the chimney. Here we have the first recorded example in the county of the new fashion in building for comfort which was to gather its greatest momentum in the reign of Elizabeth I. With this new manor house we can fittingly conclude our story of Surrey in the middle ages. Regrettably, this Tudor house, which must have been much discussed at High Table at Merton, was demolished to make way for the present edifice, mentioned on page 87.

Design of early fourteenth century floor tiles

Although Guildford was a Saxon royal manor, the west Surrey refuge against the Danes in the 10th century was Eashing, perhaps because it was considered more naturally defendable. Nevertheless, by Domesday Guildford had emerged as the main town in the western part of the county, and in the 12th and 13th centuries it was to enjoy prosperity as an important royal residence. Henry III and Edward I transacted much state business from the castle. The shell of the square keep is still well preserved on its partly artificial mound. The street topography of old Guildford suggests conscious town planning in the Saxon or early Norman period, the outline of which is basically unmodified to this day. The small medieval town was a parallelogram less than a quarter mile from east to west and about a furlong in length. Surrounding it was the 'king's dyke', a defensive ditch first mentioned in the Patent Rolls in 1274, but doubtless much older. The only principal street was High Street. This was intersected at regular intervals by narrow ways called gates, several of which still exist. By the early 14th century Guildford was a prosperous little town. The cloth industry flourished and a fair granted in 1308 on St. Catherine's Hill (where the Pilgrim's Way crossed the Wey gap), supplemented its regular markets. The presence of royalty and statesmen attracted money-lending Jews, including one Joceus, described as 'Jew of Guildford' who was murdered and robbed by thieves. Preaching friars worked amongst the poor from their friary on the north-west outskirts of the town and a charitable hospital

dedicated to St. Thomas the Martyr was established to support the sick and elderly on the east edge of the town, on a site now occupied by mock Tudor shops at the junction of the London and Epsom roads.

From the earliest surviving borough records of Guildford (1514–46) we obtain glimpses of Surrey town life at the end of the middle ages. A gild merchant regulated trade, and other courts controlled the everyday life of the town community. A court met every three weeks to curb the fraudulence of offending bakers who over-charged or gave short-weight, and that of alehouse keepers who adulterated their ale.

Periodically, the town's officers had to draft soldiers and food supplies needed for Henry VIII's military adventures and on at least one occasion (November 1544) they were required by the government to counteract a serious danger of famine by regulating the flow of grain to market. Court officials were also obliged to assess citizens for state taxes and collect on behalf of the Tudor government the money due. The courts also strove, in typical medieval fashion, to exert an exclusive control in the sphere of the cloth trade by attempting to enforce apprenticeship regulations for fullers and shearmen. In matters of general trade they carefully regulated the operation of the markets. Not all dealers were town residents: one who had a regular 'stand' was one Tykenore, a tallow chandler from Wonersh. Like all other English towns of the period, Guildford was attempting to cleanse its streets by curbing the wanderings of stray pigs. The town officials also acted as administrators for debts, and inventories of debtor's goods are invaluable insights into early town life. Poor Elizabeth Charlys, owing rent and other bills, had her household effects appraised at a value of 10s. Her chattels included three trestles, two tables, one tablecloth, a pair of sheets, her wooden platters, a candlestick and some pewter and brass, obviously the simple furnishings of a widow. James Sprenger, a debtor who had fled the town, was a painter and mason. Amongst his goods, valued at 8s., were three stones of Chalk, four little stone pots, two graining stones, 'wone potte of yello Culler' and a little supply of mustard seed, a reminder that a house painter had then to make up his own paints. Another item, 'a brokynge Booe and a narrow' was evidently the attempt of a struggling clerk to record a verbally reported 'broken bow and arrow'. Perhaps these weapons were mementoes of Sprenger's service in the king's siege of Boulogne or in the army at Portsmouth which witnessed the capsize of the ill-fated carrack *Mary Rose.*

VII Surrey as a Workshop (1560-1640)

In a letter to John Aubrey, the author of the first detailed history of Surrey, John Evelyn wrote in 1675 of the former and present industrial sites in the parish of Wotton, near Dorking, and its neighbourhood. 'Not far from my brother's house, upon the streams and ponds, since filled up and drained, stood formerly many powder mills erected by my ancestors who were the very first to bring that invention into England [to Godstone and Shere]. In this parish [of Wotton] were set up the first brass-mills for the casting, hammering into plates, cutting and drawing it into wire, that were in England . . . but the mills are removed to a further distance from my brother's house. There was likewise a fulling mill upon the same stream, now demolished, but the hammer for iron remains. These I mention because I do not remember to have seen such variety of mills and works upon so narrow a brook and in so little a compass: these being mills for corn, cloth, brass, iron and powder, etc.' Evelyn's pride in his family achievements have preserved for posterity his vivid record of industry near Wotton. Yet much the same story could have been told for the length and breadth of Surrey between 1560 and 1640, for Surrey was then a great workshop of England.

Charcoal making, seventeenth century

The most important single Surrey stream utilised to turn water-wheels was the Wandle, even though its watercourse was only nine miles long from its main source at Waddon, near Croydon, to where it entered the Thames at Wandsworth. From the first recorded history of this little stream, it has been put to work: at least 13 mills on its banks existed at Domesday. In 1610, 24 corn mills were grinding one-third of Surrey's corn supplied to London. In addition, several industrial works had developed. In 1571, for example, there is mention of a 'brazil' mill for grinding dyestuffs and fulling mills had been in operation since the 14th century. To overcome the small fall of 124ft. and the tiny volume of the stream, the Wandle millers built pen-stocked ponds for the storage of water. In 1610 they successfully resisted a proposal to divert one-tenth of the precious Wandle water to London for domestic purposes. As early as 1589 some mills comprising two wheels 'under one roof' worked eight pairs of stones and were serviced by a wooden crane lifting corn from barges.

Ironmaking

The iron industry in Surrey was not so extensive as in Sussex and Kent. Nevertheless, it was an important activity in numerous parishes during the middle ages and during the period of exceptionally rapid growth in the 16th and early 17th centuries much of the iron ore was locally worked out. Until the late 15th century iron could only be produced in small quantities at a time in simple furnaces known as bloomeries. These were built on a circular floor or hearth made of sandstone, upon which alternate layers of charcoal and ore were placed in the form of a conical heap, the whole being covered by a thick layer of clay. Hand or foot bellows were inserted into the lowermost layers of charcoal and ore in order to provide the blast. The metal collected was a spongy or pasty mass called a 'bloom', and an outlet was made at the side of the hearth to permit the removal of slag or cinder. The blooms, weighing only about 50-150lbs., were beaten into shape with hammers at a forge. From the early 15th century in Sussex such hammers were being worked by a large wheel turned by a stream of water, but no documentary evidence has yet been found for a similar development in Surrey. On the ground the visible evidence of a bloomery includes inconspicuous heaps of cinder and slag (less glassy and more 'nubbly' than that produced by the later blast furnaces), burnt clay, charcoal, and partially roasted ironstone. Such a bloomery furnace was being operated in 1354 at Tudeley in Newdigate and the mining of iron ore is mentioned at Horley Common in 1371, and on the estate of Christchurch, Canterbury in Charlwood in 1396. Very little other medieval documentary evidence has survived. It is the field archaeologist who will eventually fill in the details of medieval iron-making; the recording of sites is far from complete in Surrey. Arduous fieldwork is required because most of the surviving bloomeries are hidden along stream banks or are protected by shaws and undergrowth from the plough.

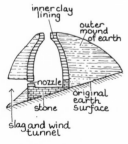

Domed iron-smelting furnace (after Henry Cleere)

In the late 15th and early 16th centuries the blast furnace was introduced from northern France to Surrey, in common with the rest of the Weald. Such furnaces were sited on relatively swift streams because their large bellows were operated by water power. Forges also used water-power hammers at this date. Streams were diverted into collecting points and waters were impounded by building earthen dams called 'bays' across the narrow valleys. On small brooks a succession of long, narrow ponds were needed as reservoirs. Many of these are now dry owing to the erosive power of a strong stream which has lowered their outlets. The 'hammer' or 'furnace' ponds that remain are amongst the most beautiful man-made features of the Weald.

52

Such furnaces consumed relatively large quantities of iron-ore. In the west Surrey Weald around Haslemere the clay ironstone occurs at a constant horizon in a narrow, crescent-shaped belt below the Horsham Stone which is the traditional roofing material in the district. The relict features of mining in the landscape are usually crater-like depressions on the ground surface between eight and 12 feet in diameter. These mark roughly infilled bell-pits, which were rarely more than 20ft. deep. Well worked-over ground is pitted with so many water-filled hollows that it looks 'as if it has suffered a bombardment'.

The calling of 'Colyer', or charcoal-burner, necessitated his living near his fire in the woods, usually in a clearing. His methods of charcoal making remained unchanged for centuries. He gathered short lengths of oak into heaps six feet high built over a hearth. The wood was then covered with turf and ashes to limit the entrance of air. The heap was then fired at several points near the bottom and a draught of air induced by leaving a hole at the top. Later the hole was covered and when the flames penetrated the heap entirely the lower holes were closed.

Iron-making

Special interest attaches to the ironworks of Witley and Thursley heaths for detailed leases have survived which include inventories of the plant and tools in use. This supplies us with the best contemporary account of the various processes employed in a Wealden ironworks. These works are described in a lease of 1610 as being 'lately erected': in 1623 they were owned by Henry Bell from whom they passed to Anthony Smith. It is the latter's lease of the ironworks to William Yalden in 1666 which is so informative. The Thursley works then comprised a furnace where the ore was reduced and cast into sows or pigs. The forge (or hammer as it was usually called in Surrey) contained two fires called the 'finery' and the 'chafery'. The sows were first converted at the finery into short, thick blooms, and then into longer ones called 'anconies'. At the chafery the roughened ends of the anconies were founded off and made ready for market. At Smith's works at Thursley there was an upper and lower finery and one chafery.

Here and there it is still possible to recapture something of the atmosphere of the era of iron-working. To visit the site of the Ewood ironworks owned by Christopher Darrell, citizen and merchant tailor of London in the mid-16th century, one turns into an old track through still remote and extensive woodland in Newdigate parish which anciently formed part of Ewood Park and provided fuel for the furnaces and forges. Across the whole width of a natural hollow created by the river Mole runs a high and massive earthen embankment (bay), over a quarter of a mile long. This impounded 'a great pond' of 90

53

Medieval glass-maker

acres, the largest pond in Surrey until it was drained in the middle of the last century. A factory now occupies its site. The upper Mole, a mere brook in dry weather but turbulent and menacing after heavy rain, is tearing down and will soon breach the dam altogether if restoration is not soon completed. A delightful low half-timbered cottage, still called Ewood Mill, stands on the downstream of the bay. This was possibly the hammerman's house, but after the iron industry ended it was converted into a corn mill (Map 7, p. 56).

Glassmaking

Another important woodland industry in Elizabethan times was glassmaking. Unlike the more important and widespread charcoal iron industry, this was localised in the Surrey and Sussex Weald, south-west of Guildford. By 1560 the centre of the industry was in the Sussex parish of Wisborough Green, but Kirdford, Chiddingfold and Hambledon were also part of the 'core' manufacturing area. In this group of parishes there is evidence of glass-making going back at least to the mid-14th century. In the late 16th century, the industry spread further to such parishes as Alfold and Ewhurst.

There is little trace of the glass industry in the present landscape. Excavated sites, usually in or near to coppice woodland, reveal merely a burnt patch and a few fragments of crucibles and glass. Only one glassmaking site has, however, been scientifically examined. It is at Blundell's Wood, Hambledon. This careful excavation tells us in some detail what a 14th-century 'glass house' was like. A wooden shed, roofed with tiles, probably covered the furnaces in which the glass was melted and annealed. Two primitive kilns, a large sub-rectangular one and a smaller 'beehive' type lay on either side of a small, round oven and a working floor. E. S. Wood has suggested that the function of the main kiln was as a melting furnace and the smaller was for 'fritting' and annealing, whilst the small oven was probably for pre-heating pots. The pottery at this site is ascribed to *c.* 1330.

The glassmakers were usually farmers using the local sands, ash and beech as a flux and oak billets to fuel the furnace. It was a craft handed down in families from generation to generation. The Peytrowes of Chiddingfold, and the Strudwicks of Kirdford were, for example, long-established glaziers. The surnames *Vitrearius* or *le Verir* occurring in 14th-century tax subsidies also probably record early practising glassmakers.

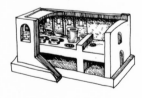

Glassmaker's crucible furnace

The rapid expansion of this historic industry in the reign of Elizabeth I is associated with improved methods of making window glass introduced from the Continent by immigrant craftsmen. A

54

number of French families are recorded in the local parish registers. The most famous amongst them is John Carré of Arras who set up as glassmaker at Fernfold *c.* 1567 to make 'Normandy and Lorraine' glass and who was buried at Alfold in 1572. Another of the Lorrainers and Normans in Surrey was Isaac Bungar (died 1643). His father probably came from France with Carré as one of those who taught Surrey folk how to make good quality window glass, then in huge demand in the fury of great rebuilding after the Reformation. Bungar is described in 1614 as 'gentleman' and owner of glass furnaces in Surrey and Sussex. He bought considerable woodland to secure fuel for his furnaces and came to monopolise production, but could not produce enough glass to satisfy the demand owing to the high cost of fuel in Surrey, forced up by the insatiable needs of glass- and iron-makers and by farmers who were beginning to use lime-kilns. He then faced, and lost, his first critical battle. A coal-fired glassmaking process was perfected by Sir Robert Mansell in Staffordshire, who enforced his monopoly of making glass in this new way so successfully that Isaac Bungar closed down his last wood-fired furnace in the Weald in 1618, after a fierce struggle. This marks the effective end of the forest glass industry in Surrey. Its most remarkable memorials are the small windows of Chiddingfold and Kirdford churches glazed with fragments of the old locally-made window glass, including many coloured pieces, which Cooper, and Hugh Kenyon, who earlier worked with Winbolt, have reconstructed.

Wooden trenchers, flour-barrel and scoop (after Gertrude Jekyll)

Clothmaking

For more than 400 years from the 13th to the 17th centuries, cloth-making was one of the staple industries of Surrey. Its former widespread distinction within the county can be pieced together from the cumulative evidence which can be drawn from probate inventories, tax lists and various deeds. Almost every Surrey village had inhabitants engaged in one or more stages in the production of woollen cloth. Caterham, Nutfield and West Horsley, by way of examples, had each their shearmen and weavers in the early 17th century. Places which by then had decayed as centres of woollen manufacture can be identified with the aid of place-names. The 'Great Teynter Field' at Kingston-upon-Thames, mentioned in a document of 1699 for instance, perpetuates the open space where the citizens laid out their cloth on racks to dry. Kingston's decline is doubtless connected with the very limited water-power available from the Hogsmill Brook. At neighbouring Mitcham, on the Wandle, the village was still busily engaged in whiting and bleaching and other

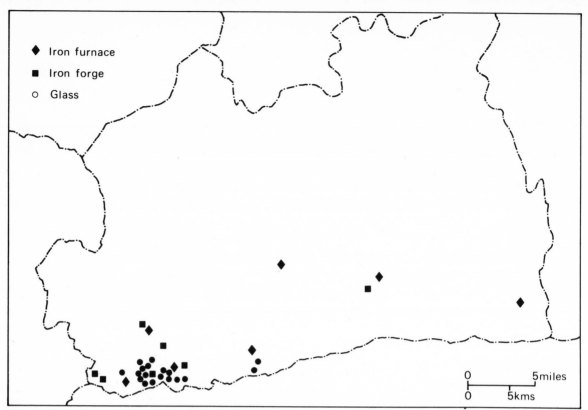

Map 7a. Surrey iron and glass making. Based on G. H. Kenyon *The Wealden Glass Industry* (1967) and E. Straker, *Wealden Iron* (1931). Townspeople kept glassworks and iron-mills at a distance because of the local rise in the cost of fuel arising from these operations. Both Kingston-upon-Thames and Guildford successfully opposed these industries in the 16th and early 17th centuries.

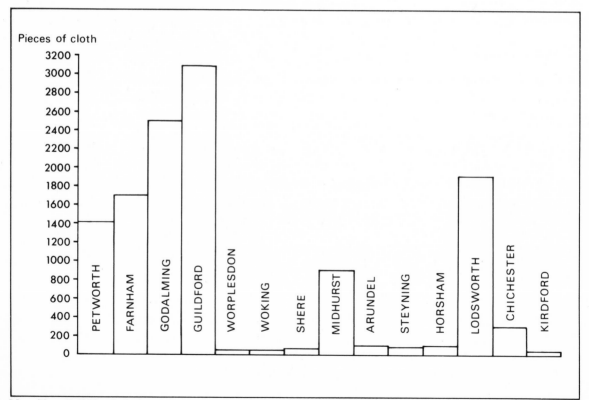

Map 7b. Guildford cloth manufacture. Data based on original ulnage returns in the Guildford Muniment Room (Loseley Ms.). The production shown represents the position in the 1570s.

finishing processes, but as the 17th century advanced Mitcham steadily abandoned the manufacture of woollen cloth for the new calico industry which throve with the rising demand for costly fabrics from wealthy London residents.

More and more the woollen cloth trade shrank in 17th-century Surrey to the towns and villages of the south-west on the fast-flowing river Wey or its many tumbling tributaries, to Farnham, Guildford, Godalming, and their outlying villages such as Ash, Shere, Stoke and Wonersh. Both Godalming and Guildford possess coats of arms bearing wool-packs, and there are innumerable inn names in Surrey which bear witness to the former trade in wool, such as 'The Woolpack' at Banstead, formerly one of the largest of Surrey sheepwalks. There is also still much visible evidence of the former clothmaking in the Surrey countryside. Many a Surrey yeoman acquired wealth and gentility from wool or cloth, and this social enhancement was expressed in domestic architecture. The most celebrated example of this kind is Crossways Farm, Abinger, the brick-fronted home of a 17th-century wool merchant. Where the cloth industry flourished villages are filled with houses built so as to take advantage of every stream for washing yarn. The houses themselves also offer clues because weavers' houses are often distinguished by their comparatively large first-floor windows which lighted the loom, or wide overhanging upper rooms which provided additional space for weaving. Yet another building device was a central balconied room set aside for weaving as at Shere and Wonersh. (Plate 12).

Spinning wheel (after Gertrude Jekyll)

Papermaking

As the cloth industry in Surrey collapsed into dereliction with the rise of new fabrics and the growing competition from more favoured centres in England drawing upon imported wools, the old fulling mills were increasingly bought up by London paper manufacturers. In the reign of James I Surrey was the leading centre in England for the manufacture of coarse brown paper used in packaging. By the end of the 17th century Surrey was also producing high-grade paper on a considerable scale. In John Evelyn's account of his visit to Byfleet paper mills in 1678 he mentions the linen being torn to shreds by pestles operated by water-power before being converted to high quality paper, and also the same operation on woollen rags destined for cheaper paper. In the finishing stage the paper was suspended on wire-trays locally produced by wire-drawing mills, themselves suffering severe competition by the end of the century from Black Country producers. By this time Godalming had become the leading Surrey paper centre.

VIII   The Improvers (1560-1640)

Sixteenth century window at Farnham (after Victoria County History)

Much of the rebuilding of Surrey between 1560 and 1640 was due to the expansion of agriculture into medieval forests, parks and other marginal lands previously turned to limited account. The rising population of both town and countryside, which increased the demand for food and consequently for land, was responsible for this development. The rapid growth of London had a particularly marked effect on land use in Surrey, it being within the ambit of the metropolitan food market. As a result, many yeoman families, as well as wealthier landowners, enjoyed increased prosperity.

Old estate maps and detailed leases enabled one to reconstruct at a local level a picture of the changing face of Surrey at this period. By way of a single example, we can trace something of the successive stages of land improvement and new buildings at Portnall Park in Egham, one of the numerous similar projects in Surrey at the time. This was the work of several generations of a yeoman family who cherished their hard-won surroundings and tried to make them habitable at the expense of that terrible antagonist, the Bagshot Sands. The Park was originally part of the royal Forest of Windsor. It was disparked before 1566 when Viscount Montague, the grandson of Sir Anthony Browne, a courtier and office holder under Henry VIII, sold it to his yeoman tenant, Henry Lane of Coworth in the adjoining parish of Old Windsor. Lane had difficulty in raising the full purchase price of £200, an event his descendants doubtless recalled when they examined their rising rent rolls and travelled over their steadily improving estate. It was Lane's son-in-law and grandson who were the main 'improvers' of Portnall, and three new tenements carved out of the Park come to our notice. 'Old House Farm' of 200 acres was originally taken in hand by Lane and his heirs. About 1646 the farmhouse was rebuilt, and in 1656 and again in 1678 the farm was let for periods of 20 years at rents of £32 and £40 per annum respectively. Clearly this was a steadily improving property of changing aspect, but the comparatively low rentals suggest that much of the acreage remained poor grazing. A second parcel of the Park, called 'New Grounds' and covering 140 acres, began its first stage of reclamation when a new farmhouse and barns were built about 1632. This poor, heathy ground was first let for an annual rent of £15, but in 1635 this was abated to £13 10s., and in 1646 reduced again to £13. The

58

rapid turnover of tenants and the very low and falling rent suggests that much of this farm was still only profitable as a rabbit warren. A third portion of the Park was let as a smallholding of 12 acres. The tenant was required to move the existing barn to a more convenient place and to modernise and enlarge the house by adding a brick chimney and two 'fire-rooms', i.e., chambers with fireplaces. This little tenement was let at £3 per annum before these improvements and at £6 afterwards. Thus even the modest land improvement at Portnall involved the rebuilding of two farmhouses and the modernising of a third: it is a story of the demand of the farmer for a more elaborate homestead that could be repeated over the length and breadth of Surrey.

The Portnall leases also give us an insight into contemporary techniques of land reclamation. The tenants were expected to denshire the heaths, that is steadily to take into cultivation by paring the bracken and furze and ploughing in ashes after burning in the manner long practised in Devon. This involved the maintenance of a lime kiln. The landlord ensured that tenants carefully preserved thorn trees, withies and selected birch trees needed for new fences but encouraged the felling of other trees to make way for crops. Birch, the most prolifically-growing tree in the Forest, provided most of the timber used on local farms and tenants were required to lop it 'as accustomedly hath been used, and not to be cut down to the ground, but to be cut in good husbandlike manner, that it may grow again'. Beech trees specifically set aside as *playsers* for providing branches used for plashing (the laying of stock fences by planting living stems or 'pleachers') were to be left unlopped. Other plantations of young birch were also to be preserved, doubtless as shelter for livestock.

Towards the end of Elizabeth's reign, marked changes in domestic architecture, representing a surge forward in comfort, became apparent in Surrey, as in most of England. The wealthy learned the cosiness of tapestried and oak-panelled rooms and the joy of a wide six-light window through which the sun poured in to flood the entire room. A staircase became a stately feature providing an easy access to rooms newly built over the medieval open hall, an improvement made possible by collecting smoke that had formerly escaped through the rafters and gablets of the hall, by chimneys or smoke bays. With increasing prosperity there was also a desire to enlarge the house, normally achieved by demolishing two end bays and building a cross wing which then provided the best living rooms. This period of change is unparalleled in history of the English house.

Surrey possesses some of the finest examples of old brick, half-timbered cottages that it is possible to find in any English county.

Seventeenth-century wood brackets

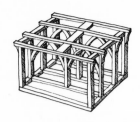

Timber construction of Church House, West Horsley

Even within a mile of the perimeter of Gatwick airport, amidst some of the most drastic landscape changes, are more than a score of 15th- and 16th-century houses, some heavily disguised in 18th-century or even modern fronts upon the vast strength of their native oak beams. In the parish of West Horsley there are half a dozen half-timbered houses along The Street and another cluster of yeoman's farmsteads further afield. Other rewarding parishes of similar richness are Bramley and Shamley Green. John Baker has estimated that in Surrey as a whole there is an average of over two early half-timbered houses in a square mile. Their survival ensures that people will not be strangers to Surrey's organic historical growth.

Even at Charlwood in the deep Surrey Weald, the modernisation of Pixton's was as early as 1571 and new houses with chimneys were being built by the end of Elizabeth's reign, such as Charlwood Place Farm. Numerous yeoman's houses renovated before 1600 were not provided with a chimney stack, presumably on account of expense, but with a specially constructed smoke-bay. One of the finest and best-known examples of a 15th-century house altered in the 16th and 17th centuries is Unstead Manor House, Bramley. The evolution of this house has followed a standard sequence. The earliest surviving parts are an open hall house of about 1400. The hall formerly extended farther to the right. The door and carved lintel are probably original. The lovely crown-post roof and soot-blackened rafters indicate that the hall was formerly open to the roof. The centre crown-post was moulded and carved by a medieval carpenter with some care, because it would have been the main decorative feature in the centre of the open roof of the house. The cross-wing at Unstead was added about 1600 on the site of one room of the medieval house. The struts and braces in its upper part served a decorative as well as a structural purpose. Its fireplaces were carved in a form of hard Chalk, a common characteristic of early Surrey houses.

Another fine half-timbered house illustrating the great social changes taking place in 16th- and 17th-century Surrey is Nursecombe in Bramley. A cross-wing was added to the medieval hall house, the hall was floored over, and a chimney added *c.*1500. A further cross-wing was added *c.*1620 to provide a 'great parlour'. This turned it into a comfortable yeoman's farmstead with a dairy, buttery wash and brew house, all of which services were originally provided by the medieval kitchen (Plate 6).

A seventeenth century leaded casement from near Godalming (after Gertrude Jekyll)

Moving up the social scale the houses built or enlarged by the iron-masters greatly embellish the present Surrey scene. The ironmasters were generally accounted members of the local gentry and their houses equalled, or surpassed, contemporary manor houses. One was

60

'Rake', the house owned by Bell and Smith, who were the Thursley ironmasters. This is a good specimen of an Elizabethan house. It has a panelled parlour containing a very delicately carved oak mantelpiece bearing the initials H.B. (for Henry Bell), and the date 1602, but its most important structural feature is the staircase which is evidently a transition between the earliest stairs winding round a newel or within solid walls and the later and more practical one of a square plan with newels and balustrades. Another house greatly improved by a flourishing ironmaster was 'Burningfold' in Dunsfold, the home of Richard Marche, owner of Dunsfold furnace at the end of the 16th century. Its nucleus was a medieval hall house with the standard open hall, offices and solar, or sleeping room. Marche provided a fine new front, of a design similar to that of nearby Tangley Manor and dated 1582, and inserted rooms into the first floor, served by a plain winding newel oak staircase.

Turning now to gentlemen's mansions, one of the earliest and most exquisite achievements was Sutton Place, built by Sir Richard Weston, an intimate member of Henry VIII's court, *c*. 1523-5. The design was probably influenced by the châteaux Weston had observed on his travels on the king's business in the country of the Loire, then the centre of artistic life in France. Sutton Place is built in brick and terra-cotta around a quadrangle enclosing a space of 81 ft. on each side and fronted by an arched gateway and flanked by lofty hexagonal towers. It survives as one of the best examples of an early type of country house of the Surrey landed gentleman.

After Sutton Place a spate of building began in Surrey. The king himself was an enthusiastic builder at Hampton Court, Nonsuch Palace and Oatlands. A new development in Surrey is marked by Loseley, built in 1561-9 by Sir William More. This was the first Surrey mansion laid out on an H- or E-shaped plan which set the fashion for two generations and more, and is characteristic of Elizabethan domestic architecture in both Surrey and Sussex. The north wing of the house containing the main apartments still survives.

It is instructive to examine an inventory of the contents of a gentleman's house in Elizabeth's reign. It relates to Beddington Manor, the home of Sir Francis Carew. The furniture in the parlour, the main living room, included new luxuries such as Turkey and Venetian carpets and no less than 18 paintings, but it was sparsely and rather uncomfortably furnished. Ten 'joyned stoulles' and two leather chairs, one long table and one small table completed the main living room furniture. The 'great chamber', or main bedroom, contained only the bedstead, a chair in satin and a 'great wenscote

Typical early seventeenth century newel stair-case, Shoelands, Puttenham. (after Victoria County History)

61

Old Cottage fire-place

cheast' and, although the bed hangings were richly woven and embroidered, there is still little variety in furniture. Although living standards were noticeably rising in 16th-century Surrey, there is still a note of marked austerity.

The small farmer continued to live frugally, as is suggested by the inventory of goods of John Potter, a farmer of Thorpe who died in 1637. His primary implements were a horse-drawn plough and a pair of harrows and his dung-cart. A flitch of bacon was in store and 3 sows, 2 hogs, 2 yearling bullocks and two calves and 18 acres under corn constituted his only wealth. His house comprised hall, kitchen and chamber with loft above. In the hall were merely a cupboard (perhaps under the stairs), one long table, a chair, a stool and a form, evidently for himself, his wife and his children respectively. In his kitchen was the traditional fireplace with its brass pots, kettles, fire shovel, pair of tongs, pot-hanger, spit and grid-iron. The bedstead and two chests were the only furnishings in the chamber, and the loft contained 'bedsteadles', that is bunks for the children or his labourers.

Plague and Other Epidemics

The local community engaged in Surrey agriculture and industry was far more subject to natural and civil catastrophe than it is today. Bermondsey in the 16th and early 17th centuries was particularly prone to epidemics, presumably on account of its congested streets and proximity to London. Between 1555 and 1608 heavy mortality occurred on three occasions—in September and October 1563 (169 burials in the parish churchyard), August and September 1593 (150 burials), and in the terrible catastrophe of July to September 1603 when 500 inhabitants died. These death rolls, compiled from the extant parish registers, are to be compared with an average of 20–25 burials each month. The epidemic of 1603 took off scores of children and adolescents as also did a less severe outbreak in 1608: diphtheria or scarlet fever may have been responsible. Paupers were also particuarly vulnerable to disease, but the healthy and strong of each generation were clearly cut back repeatedly by epidemics. In the countryside the incidence of plague and other epidemics was less severe but still virulent. The Dorking parish registers reveal comparatively large death rolls in 1563, 1593, 1603 and 1610, and those of Charlwood, a Wealden parish, tell much the same story. Nineteen persons died here of plague in less than three months in 1610, and several families suffered severely. Mortlake escaped the epidemic disease of 1603 and 1610 but suffered dreadfully from the Plague of 1665, 205 of the villagers dying in that year, 65 in the month of September alone.

62

IX The Surrey of John Evelyn (1640-1740)

To John Evelyn, diarist, founding member of the Royal Society, connoisseur, writer and landscapist, Surrey was 'the country of my Birth and my Delight'. As a representative of the 17th century, he brings before us in every word the atmosphere and setting of his age. He shared intensely the deep affection for Italian art, sculpture and architecture which was the prevailing mood of England during his lifetime and also the new fashions emanating from France and the Low Countries. He expressed these in the connoisseurship of architecture, painting, medals and also in the laying-out of gardens. In these tastes he was one of a group of perceptive patrons and collectors, many resident in great houses on the banks of the Thames and its environs, whose avid enthusiasm for Renaissance and contemporary works of art from the reign of James I plunged all Surrey into the mainstream of European taste.

Evelyn also shared the growing interest in agriculture which was the mark of the English gentleman of his day, and through his friendship with Henry Capel (whose important garden was the beginning of Kew's horticultural fame) he became interested in botany and more and more absorbed in trees. His favourite tree species were those most characteristic of Surrey, the discoveries of his youth in his own wooded environment at Wotton, near Dorking. These included the oak, ash, elm and beech amongst the timber trees. In nothing, however, does Evelyn better communicate the spirit of the Surrey countryside than in his relish for its native evergreens— holly, yew, privet and box—which, before the introduction of exotics into England, provided the only greenery offsetting the bareness of the English winter. A holly hedge, 'glitt'ring with its arm'd and varnish'd leaves' was to him a most glorious and refreshing object.

Moreover, Evelyn interested himself in his own part of Surrey in the acclimatisation of fir and pine, which brought with them a fancy of the Italian landscape. It would be difficult to find lovelier woodland scenery anywhere in England than that in the 'Evelyn country' between Guildford and Dorking, on once barren Sands and thin Chalk soils. Here the pinewoods are generally acknowledged to be an enrichment of Surrey landscape. Most of the planting is not earlier in origin than the late 18th century, but the thick pinewoods which run up from

The old tithe barn, Witley, converted into a handsome dwelling

63

*Typical barn and 'hovel'
of an old Surrey farm.
(after Singleton Open Air
Museum)*

Evelyn's home to the top of Leith Hill probably sprang in part from Evelyn's own planting a century earlier.

His lifelong interest in forestry and woodcrafts led to successive editions of *Sylva*, the book on tree culture for which, after his *Diary*, he is now chiefly remembered. Amongst communities more provident and self-sufficient than our own, craftsmen carefully put the varied working qualities of timber trees to the best use. The ash supplied husbandmen with carts, ladders and ploughs. Elm was used for timber immersed in water, as for mills, ladles and ship's planks below the water line; the joiner prized walnut for its fine graining and colour, and the gunsmith and coachmaker used it to make stocks and hoops respectively: from holly was made handles—stocks for tools, door-bars and bolts (for wood served in the 17th century many purposes for which wrought iron was later used). The close-grained hornbeam was used for sundry mechanical purposes now chiefly served by metal castings. The box, one of the most characteristic of Surrey trees, was of remarkably varied use to the turner, engraver, carver, mathematical instrument, comb and pipe-makers.

In his *Diary* Evelyn kept a methodical record of all the visits he made to country seats for the purpose of viewing pictures, architecture, gardens or plantations. One can weave a history of Surrey around his travels. Let us in imagination accompany him on a tour of Surrey in the 1680s calling at the country houses with which he had the closest association. From his town house in Dover Street, a short journey over London Bridge would have brought him to 'paradisical Clapham' where people then lived very 'handsomely' in large houses upon the Common. Clapham's social *cachet* in the second half of the 17th century was magnetic; it drew in, for example, Samuel Pepys towards the close of his life. Wandsworth would have come next on the road westwards out of London, a place most notable for its brass mills worked by water-power, but it was not yet sufficiently industralised to have driven out the gentry and citizens of London that still clung there. At Sheen were Sir William Temple's famous orangeries 'kept in the Holland way' and well-stocked fruit gardens. From here Temple wrote several famous works, including his discovery that the hugeness of built-up London raised the air temperatures of the surrounding countryside, thus making it particularly suitable for tender fruits (Plate 22).

Evelyn could not have resisted Ham House 'inferior to few of the best villas in Italy itself' (though he frowned at the extravagant living of its inmates), or the grounds of Hampton Court then being newly laid out in great avenues of chestnuts, fountains, parterres, all in the formal French style of Le Nôtre. Turning away reluctantly from the Thames riverside he would have kept a sharp eye for the dark masses of

Clandon Park

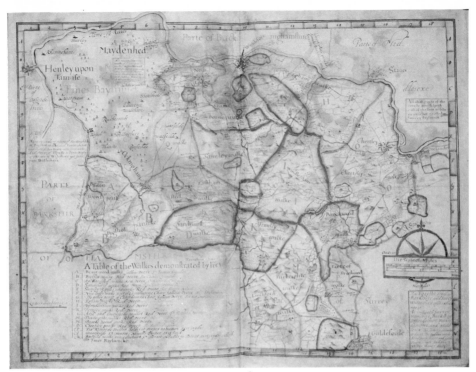

18. John Norden's map of the Royal Forest of Windsor (1607). The Surrey Bailiwick brought local farmers into close touch with the Crown. Elizabeth exempted the men of Pirbright from the obligation of providing provender for the royal horses in compensation for the damage done to their crops by deer. James I, a keen huntsman, threatened to prohibit swine-grazing in the Forest unless holes dug by rootling pigs were regularly filled in.

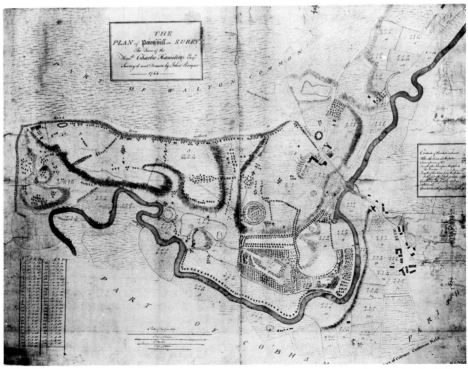

19. John Rocque's plan of Pains Hill, 1754. This shows the early work of William Hamilton.

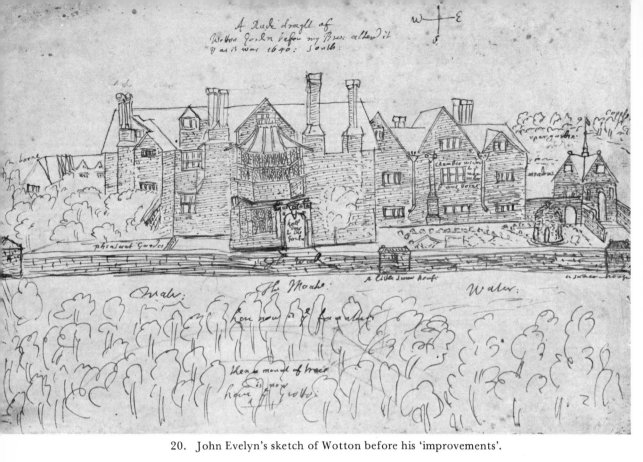

20. John Evelyn's sketch of Wotton before his 'improvements'.

21. George Lambert's *Wotton Park* (1739), showing John Evelyn's landscaping. The then owner carried on in his grandfather's tradition. To a correspondent at West Horsley who requested beech plants he wrote: '. . . for fir seed in my opinion you need go no further, the trees of my raising being the best in my observation as flourishing as any I have seen in this country'.

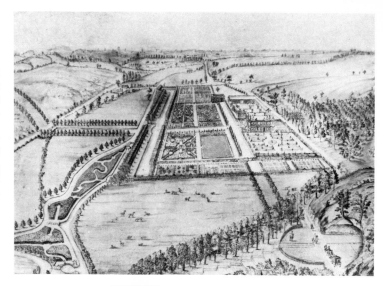

22. Moor Park, Farnham, c.1690, the home of the highly accomplished Sir William Temple. In his retirement he indulged in gardening, a lifelong passion and completed his essay *Of Gardens*. He created at Moor Park an earthly paradise according to the notion of his day with parterres, long terraces, retaining walls, formal canals, pleached alleys and gazebos.

23. Wanborough House, the home of Morris Birkbeck.

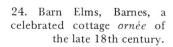

24. Barn Elms, Barnes, a celebrated cottage *ornée* of the late 18th century.

25. An aerial view of Farnham. For the town-planner, architect, or anyone concerned with the development of land and buildings, Farnham offers an ideal blueprint of a pleasant, urban environment of dignity and charm.

'goodly woods' and the glint of water interspersed between orchards which he considered to be peculiarly Surrey, and also for the tree avenues, greenhouses (then called 'Stovers', from the Dutch), orangeries and vineries which were spring up at every seat. Southwards, Box Hill was reached. Its attraction to Evelyn was probably less in the panorama it afforded than the pleasant walks through its box, yew and juniper groves, which made Evelyn fancy being transported 'into some new or enchanted country'. The famous walnut trees of Norbury, then a low-lying mansion near the river, earned his attention, as did Deepdene, also near Dorking, then notable for its 'amphitheatre' garden of exotics. In his traverses of the North Downs he repeatedly observed how the wooded and higher parts were then being much improved for arable farming by the method of denshiring. Much of the Chalk had been merely used previously for rabbit warrens like the great Borough Warren in Banstead. Even in the Weald there was marked agricultural improvement. Aubrey writes of Capel: 'This parish more naturally produced wood than corn or grass and was formerly so ill-cultivated that had not the inhabitants supplied their want of corn from their neighbouring markets, they might have eaten acorns instead of bread; but as they have now learned the art of improving their land by manuring it with lime or chalk they now have a surplus of grain'. Nearer home Evelyn often called at Sutton Farm in Shere, the home of his friend, Peter Hussey. 'He is the neatest husband for curious ordering his domestic and field accommodations and what pertains to husbandry, that I have ever seen, as to granaries, tacklings, tools and utensils, ploughs, carts, stables, wood-piles, woodhouses, even to hen-roosts and hog-troughs. Methinks I saw Old Cato or Varro in him; all substantial, all in exact order.' Evelyn himself fulfilled in no small degree his own vision of the ideal farmer.

In *Memories for my grandson*, begun in 1704 and written for the edification of his young heir when Evelyn was 84 years old, he advised on the management of the Wotton estate. This is a most vivid account of the life and attitudes of a Surrey country gentleman at the end of the 17th century and gives us a fascinating glimpse of everyday life at Wotton after three generations of family endeavour, as well as being a window into Evelyn's mind. Evelyn is revealed as a very tight-fisted economist who enthusiastically concerned himself in the day-to-day routine of his home, farm, gardens, orchards and woodlands, and who farmed and planted for a vision of England rather than for immediate profit. He shrewdly recommended the tree-planting of timber trees (oak, ash, or elm) as 'the only best and proper Husbandry the Estate is capable of . . .'. To prevent further reckless destruction of the old forests he ordered his grandson to stoke his stoves with peat dug on the estate, or with sea coal.

Polesden Lacey, the old house (built 1631-32) and demolished c.1818

65

The landscaping by the brothers Evelyn which made Wotton the most famous garden in England in the mid-17th century is recorded by John Evelyn in the *Diary* and in his own etchings. John Evelyn's first garden alterations were made when he was only 23 years old in 1643, after the death of his father, and on his return from his first continental tour. 'I built, by my brother's permission, a study, made a fish-pond, an island, and some other solitudes and retirements at Wotton', he wrote. The main reshaping at Wotton appears to have been in 1652–3 when the Civil War was over and John Evelyn had made a Grand Tour embracing Italy and Paris. With his brother's willing help, John then became engrossed in furnishing Wotton with 'all the amenities of a villa and garden after the Italian manner . . .'. John's role appears to have been as adviser : 'I went with my brother Evelyn to Wotton to give him what directions I was able about his garden'. George Evelyn then reshaped Wotton on the lines which have basically survived to this day. He dug into the side of the sand hill overshadowing the house on the south for the site of parterres. The spoil filled the moat. The steep hill was terraced, a fountain was supplied by an aqueduct from the river Tillingbourne, and a tree-covered mount was fashioned above a splendid temple. An avenue of Spanish chestnut trees, then 'all the mode for the avenues to their country places in France', extended southwards towards Leith Hill and several grottoes were provided. A *Hortus hyemalis,* or winter garden, prepared with plants that John Evelyn had brought back from Padua, was also added. Many of his brother's alterations are shown as annotations on John Evelyn's etching of the grounds in 1640 and by a fine drawing of Wotton garden in 1653, which shows the finished work near the house (Plates 20 and 21).

Another famous garden designed on Italian lines by John Evelyn was at Albury Park. Under 1667, John Evelyn entered in his *Diary*: 'I accompanied Mr. Howard to his villa at Albury, where I designed for him the plot of his canal and garden, with a crypt through the hill'. He returned three years later to find the canal under construction and the vineyard planted as he had designed it and the then unique crypt (called by Evelyn a 'Pausilippe' from the name of the subterranean passage from the famous Grotto di Posilippo near Naples) dug through the hill. All this was to thrill William Cobbett more than 150 years later, especially the terrace, a quarter of a mile long, backed by its yew hedge. 'Take it altogether, this certainly is the prettiest garden that I ever beheld. There was taste and sound judgement at every step in the laying out of the place. Everywhere utility and convenience is combined with beauty.'

Seventeenth century timber-work at Crowhurst Place. (after Victoria County History)

66

X The Age of Luxury (1640-1740)

After the Restoration in 1660 and still more so from the Revolution in 1688, the wealth of England notably increased, and kings, princes, noblemen and gentry vied with each other in erecting houses of ever-increasing splendour. Under these influences London extended more than at any time in its previous history, foreshadowing everything that was to come. As early as 1629 the artist-ambassador Rubens had marvelled at the size and grandeur of London's 'outward cincture'. It was from Inigo Jones that wealthy Londoners derived their avid taste for continental architecture, landscape design, painting and sculpture. A distinctive characteristic of this development was the beauty of country houses on the rural margins of London. Travelling from the coast on the old Lewes road in the 1720s, one would have encountered the first houses of London citizens at Carshalton; fine large mansions, looking more like the seats of the nobility rather than country houses of citizens and merchants. From the wooded hillside of still rural Mitcham, the hayfields of Clapham, Streatham and Tooting could be seen similarly invaded by large mansions. From the rising ground of Clapham the view eastwards took in the market gardens and fields of Camberwell and Peckham, containing some of the finest houses outside London itself, and westwards, towards Coombe and Kingston (Plate 14), the wooded country was similarly bespangled with new buildings. Camberwell and other villages near London were, in fact, shedding their old half-timbered houses for handsome modern ones in brick, built to high standards of quality and design. As early as 1661 a lease of land stipulated that in place of an 'old ruinous messuage' fronting on the road at Camberwell church was to be built a brick house with 'fire chimneys' on well constructed foundations and with a ceiling height of eight feet for the principal rooms. The house was to be set back in the orchard of the old house and a brick wall constructed to embellish it. The specification for this dwelling epitomises the architectural change in domestic building which was to transform the entire face of Surrey on the fringe of London, bringing with it periwigged and be-powdered citizens into Surrey's countryside (Plate 5).

The finest houses of all, more like palaces than houses, had begun to line the Thames between Chelsea and Weybridge. 'England never had such a glorious show to make in the world before', wrote Defoe.

Lancelot 'Capability' Brown

Ham House, based on engraving by Turner after N. Whittock

Horace Walpole, who hated country life, lamented this rural extension of London into Surrey and Middlesex. 'Think what London would be if the chief houses were in it, as in the cities of other countries, and not dispersed like a great rarity of plums in a vast pudding of country'. This fury of building is one of the earliest manifestations of that deeply-rooted British preference for country life which distinguished London from continental cities such as Amsterdam, Paris, Bologna and Florence, and was destined to reshape Surrey landscape and its society. The *nouveaux riches* craved for a country house in which to spend the summer months (the roads were too miry in winter to make a permanent residence feasible), 'to draw their breath in a clean aire' before returning for the winter to the 'Smoke and Dirt, Sin and Seacoal' of the busy city (Plate 24).

The houses built under these cultural and social influences have been described on numerous occasions and no useful purpose would be served by detailed repetition here. The Thames-side house at Ham deserves special recognition for it remains alone in Surrey as a 17th-century house with contents that have survived to a remarkable degree intact. Its rooms (open to the public by the National Trust) are not so much 'period' rooms as original and substantial works of art in their own right. Entering Ham House one savours to the full the atmosphere and spirit of the late 17th century. Its rooms are small, in the fashion of the time, but are lavishly furnished (in great contrast to the plainness of even an important room of an Elizabethan house) with profuse French-style furniture and all sorts of original hangings—velvet, brocade, damask—fringed with silk in silver and gold. Nothing is so vividly expressive of the 'politer but ruinously expensive way of life' introduced into Surrey after the Restoration than the remarkable survival of Ham House (Frontispiece and Plate 15).

All this was the work of Elizabeth Dysart and her second husband, created Duke of Lauderdale in 1672. They extended and modernised the house built in 1610 and furnished it with luxuries remarkable even in that lavish age to match their ambitious rôle in Restoration political and social life. They bounded the grounds with a canal leading into the Thames by a water-gate, as in the manner of the perfect French villas on the river Loire or the style of Dutch patricians' houses on the river Vecht, and laid out a formal garden in the French mode with a parterre extending to a square lawn divided by side gravel paths which led to a 'wilderness' on a cart-wheel plan. In all but detail the garden (though not the canal which also deserves re-creation) has survived and it is being restored by the National Trust according to an original plan of 1670 still hanging in the house. The garden will again soon be like 'a matching saucer to a beautiful cup'.

The fashion for building country houses was not only stimulated by the general desire for outdoor recreation and repose. There was also a growing appreciation of ideal forms of landscape, largely through the medium of Claude Lorrain's and Poussin's transcripts of scenery around Rome and Tivoli. Travellers began to report that the soft, flowing and rounded lines of Surrey scenery, the smoothness and fatness of its garden-like fields, and the lushness of its greenery were reminiscent of such 'classical scenery'. The first Surrey scene to be published by those curious of landscape was the view from Cooper's Hill above Runnymede on the Thames, made illustrious by John Denham's poem written in 1643. James Thomson's *The Seasons* (1738) gave added publicity to the 'soft windings of the great Mole' near Esher. In the early 18th century the more inaccessible Surrey prospects were still virtually unknown. The earliest surviving appreciation of the Surrey man-made landscape stretching out panoramically below Leith Hill dates from 1717 when John Dennis considered that the trim, varied and orderly countryside was not to be surpassed anywhere in Europe (Plate 30).

Late 18th-century town houses, Farnham

It was in the 17th century that the North Downs first acquired a reputation as a health resort and place of recreation. Banstead's medical fame was evidently brief for by Aubrey's day London physicians no longer prescribed its 'wholesome air', preferring to send patients to the neighbouring spa at Epsom, or to Cotmandean, near Dorking, where Defoe noted that 'some learned physicians have singled out as the best air in England'. Banstead and its downland, however, continued to hold the affections of wealthy London families as a sporting centre. John Tolland (1711) regarded its downs as the finest in the world, 'being covered with grass finer than Persian carpets and perfumed with wild thyme and juniper'. This mat of soft, springy grass was admirable for riding, hunting, shooting and horse-racing, all sports practised with ever-growing indulgence by leisure-lovers in post-Restoration London. Banstead and Epsom became the acknowledged Cockney paradise. Both had racecourses and abundant facilities for physical exercise.

Epsom's chief claim to fame was a spa. Its heyday was brief. The origins of Epsom Spa can be traced to the early 17th century, but it does not appear to have become popular until after the Restoration, when the age was more completely identified with pleasure. Pepys, Dorothy Osborne and Celia Fiennes and many others have recorded their impressions. For the appearance of this infant spa, we can draw upon an excellent engraving by William Schellinks (drawn 1662). (Plate 13). Apparently, Epsom was still primarily a medical centre with few facilities for taking the waters; what little was available in the way of social facilities was in the village, a quarter of a mile away.

Wooden dairying utensils (after Gertrude Jekyll)

Tolland tells us in 1711 that the old wells on Epsom Common (depicted in Schellink's drawing) were then less regarded than new wells established on the western edge of Epsom itself. In the meantime, a reception room had been built at the old wells; this was demolished in 1804, by which time Epsom had long since ceased to be a spa. Tolland gives an admirable account of the new wells and the growing town of Epsom which had sprung up around them. It appears to have been a veritable 'garden-city'. Tastefully ornamented houses spread along a tree-lined avenue shaped in the form of a crescent, a mile in length. Many houses had arbours of clipped yew or box and under these the summer residents took their ease with 'a cheerful glass and a pipe'. Epsom Spa was clearly no more a part of Surrey than Brighton was to become part of Sussex. 'By the conversation of those who walk here', added Tolland, 'you would fancy yourself on the Exchange at St. James', or in an East India factory, or with the army in Flanders.' Here Whig and Tory patrons ignored their political prejudices and joined fraternally in gossip. Bowling greens provided recreation in the mornings. An orchestra played in the afternoons, and a ball was held most evenings. Above the town was the Ring, a high part of the Downs where on Sunday evenings as many as 60 coaches would gather for the sake of the view.

All this luxury was generating handicrafts and industry on the south bank of the Thames. Rocque's 1746 *Survey of London* shows Southwark as a huddle of closely-built houses and streets, separated by the tenter-grounds where newly-woven calicoes were stretched out on hooks to settle evenly into shape on the drying poles (tenters). The Tower of London and St. Paul's Cathedral (not long rebuilt) stood out across the river; to the west lay Lambeth Marsh, still uncrossed by the imminent approach roads to the projected Westminster Bridge; to the south all was open country. Southwark was a community of its own, cut off from the main body of the metropolis save for London Bridge used by local craftsmen when visiting their guildhalls. Southwark was by now well established as a home of immigrants. Since the 16th century, refugees from Flanders, Holland and France, exiled for their religious beliefs, had settled here, bringing their independence, ideals and skills and turning Southwark into a centre of the weaving and stone-cutting industry and religious nonconformity. On the river-front were the wharves, coal and timber yards. Behind these along Gravel Lane, Love Lane, Angel Lane, Dirty Lane, Orange Street, Lemon Street and Melancholy Lane, were the cloth factories, vinegar makers, glass houses and stonemason's yards that employed the local inhabitants.

XI The Remaking of the Road System and New Forms of Transport (to 1840)

Until the late 18th century Surrey had no effective means of communication between its neighbouring towns. So appalling were the ways across the Surrey Weald, especially in West Surrey, that for several months of the year farmers had no ready access to markets. John Burton's travel through Surrey and Sussex *c.* 1730 was made memorable by his arduous journey over the clays. William Cobbett encountered the deepest clay he had ever experienced at Ewhurst. In the words of another contemporary observer, wagons dragged along by some means or another through the Weald Clay were abandoned the whole winter if they stuck in the autumn mires. John Mechi, a successful businessman and reforming farmer, never forgot his father's struggles early in the 19th century to convey his corn to Guildford market by pack-horse along rough bridle-roads, impassable to wheeled traffic. In wet weather such ways were also utterly unusable by horse. On the drier ridges the going was easier but linking by-roads over the soft rocks of the Chalk or Lower Greensand ridge were hollowed out into deeply-rutted narrow tracks along which the saddle-horse was normally the only practicable form of transport. Away from the market towns generally the roads deteriorated and horse-riders abandoned them for a course over farmland. Even on the margins of London the badness of the ways near Epsom had emptied the Spa of its visitors in autumn. Thus long stretches of Surrey roads before the Age of Improvement were not usable as wagon or carriage-ways, and a regular service of carriers was non-existent.

By the mid-18th century these deficiencies were acknowledged to be a great obstacle to economic advancement. A necessity began to be felt for better means of communication, especially between London and the coast, for which no good routes existed. Population was rising, but the lack of good roads prevented farmers making the optimum use of land. The mid-18th century also witnessed the advent of the coaching era. The wealthy became travellers, craving for ever greater mobility. Surrey, as has been related, was becoming a favoured place of residence by people who required convenient access to London. Their carriage-wheels pressed hard upon the heels of the roadmakers, and new mansions sprang up along ways provided with smooth, hard, surfaces. Moreover, Surrey came to lie athwart two of the busiest routes in the whole of England; to Portsmouth, an

Bonnetted freight waggon —early nineteenth century (after J. M. W. Turner)

71

Sussex and Surrey waggoner in the Borough, Southwark

increasingly important naval base, and to Brighton and other seaside resort towns, which from the social movement of sea bathing for health became fashionable amongst the wealthy. These resorts required for success new roads providing direct access to London. To this end the various Turnpike trusts competed with one another to provide the best road services, the easiest gradients, the most direct and best hostelleried routes between main towns and London. This competition had by 1820 created the best road system in Europe.

The successive developments of this new road system tell a particularly fascinating story in Surrey because by the then rising standards of road transport many stretches of its roads were considered too slow or unsafe for stage coaches driven at the ever-faster speeds in vogue. The lie of the land was a basic cause of difficulty. For generations travellers by saddle-horse had instinctively made for higher ground on the ridgeways. This was responsible for steep gradients and circuitous courses around hillsides which were obviated by direct and better graded new routes. Hence the county furnishes many instances of the abandonment of long stretches of former roads. These derelict ways are one of the most distinctive and charming features of the Surrey landscape.

Britannia Depicta (1720), an improved edition of Ogilby's road-book, records only four high roads traversing appreciative stretches of Surrey. Of these two, the Portsmouth and the Old Lewes roads were very ancient lines of communication. The latter ran first to Croydon, then followed the Caterham valley, and thence over the Chalk escarpment to Godstone where, unlike the present road, it took the direct line over Tilburstow Hill. This road, in Aubrey's phrase, was 'the great road into Sussex'. Besides Lewes, the ancient ports of Shoreham and Pevensey were served by branches of this road, and in the mid-18th century it became one of the routes to the young seaside resort of Brighton. A third road marked in *Britannia Depicta* was from London to Arundel which ran from Epsom over the Mickleham Downs to Dorking and thence over the sand hills by Coldharbour, to fall steeply from Leith Hill just west of Anstiebury Camp. The fourth route was the cross-road from Godalming on the Portsmouth road to Petworth and Chichester. This climbed steeply out of the Wey Valley and ran over hilly country to Hambledon Common.

This dearth of public roads was replaced within a century by virtually a new system of direct trunk routes between London and the coast and also by a close network of cross-country connections. The first stretch of Surrey road to be improved was the 10 miles between Reigate and Crawley, authorised in 1696 as a saddle-horse road and not improved for carriages until 1755. In 1820 this stretch was again improved by lowering the gradient of Reigate Hill, piercing a sand ridge at Reigate by a tunnel and by a more direct route between Sidlow Bridge and Povey Cross. The deserted older route can be traced curving to the east over Horse Hill and this still remained the only practical way when the river Mole was in flood. These and similar improvements to 'Cockney highways' were stigmatised by William Cobbett in his familiar measured terms.

Various other coaching roads through Surrey were made to Brighton. The old way, via Godstone, for example, was improved by avoiding the climb over Tilburstow Hill. An alternative route was by Epsom, Dorking and Horsham. The Vale of Mickleham first became an important thoroughfare on this route in 1755 when the road between Epsom and Horsham was turnpiked. In earlier times the 'winter' road to London was so frequently obstructed by the flooding of the river Mole that coachmen and carriers preferred to come over the North Downs by way of Sutton and Betchworth. Another improved coast road was the hilly Dorking–Coldharbour stretch, abandoned for a fine new route over the Holmwood (the present A.23 road). The alternative road (regularly used in Evelyn's day) up Wolven's lane and over the Chalk escarpment to Leatherhead was abandoned at the same time. The new road authorised in 1764 between Milford and Chidding-fold left completely deserted the stretch between Hambledon Common and North Bridge.

The main alteration to the Portsmouth road was between Thursley and Hindhead in 1826. The old track will be found by Thursley Church. Another interesting new coaching road in Surrey was that made from Epsom to Guildford under Acts of 1755-8. The new road ran directly across the fields, leaving the villages along the springline connected by the superseded loops of the old road. The continuation of this road from Guildford to Farnham resulted in the abandonment in 1758 of the steep grass-grown track expressively known as 'The Mount'.

These were some of the smooth Surrey roads along which the stage coaches 'raced' at 12 miles per hour, leaving only 20 minutes on the road for passengers to snatch a hurriedly-eaten but gargantuan meal in the staging inns on the route. Despite the building of railways they carried little local goods traffic until the 1870s. Until this time, for example, the Dorking and Epsom carrier made his regular journeys through Surrey villages to and from the *George* inn in the Borough, the enthrallingly noisy scene commemorated by Dickens.

Although main highways were subject to improvement, the local parish roads remained deplorable. James Malcolm's *Compendium of modern husbandry* (1805) lists Surrey parishes with local roads as bad as 'some of the most inaccessible and uninhabited parts of Ireland' included not only most of the Weald parishes, but even those linking well-

Reigate, archway covering improved road to London

*Ornamental cottages,
Ockley, c.1840*

filled villages on the edge of London such as Camberwell, Peckham, Wandsworth, and in the Kingston district. Much of the Surrey Weald still remained inaccessible in the 1830s and 1840s when the first railway proposals were being debated. All around the central Low Weald between Dorking, Horsham and East Grinstead there was a want of local roads which prevented travel in wet weather. The land was still only half cultivated owing to the expense of the carriage of indispensable lime and, although it produced excellent timber, there was no adequate means of carrying it away, so extremely bad were the roads. Farmers were placed at a disadvantage in several other ways. Wheat from this district, for example, fetched lower prices at Horsham than at Guildford market because Horsham had no water carriage and it was estimated that fat steers walked to Smithfield in the traditional way 'on the hoof' lost 3–4 per cent. in weight during the journey. The economic effects of good turnpikes on Surrey agriculture must not, therefore, be over-estimated; not until railways were built and the local roads were effectively improved could most farmers really take full advantage of the nearness to London.

The historian also needs to take into account the very varying physical condition and management of the respective administrative divisions of turnpikes (Map 8, p. 75).

Malcolm noted that 'if roads do not happen to lead to a gentleman's house, in the worse order and more impassable are they, and the lower will be the rents of the farms'. His observation that in Surrey generally rents fell within increasing distance to London, those of farms within the innermost ring of up to an half-hour's drive from Stone's End in Kennington being almost double the rentals in an outer zone of up to one hour's distance and six times as much as those in remoter parts, anticipates von Thünen's well-known doctrine of the economic zoning by rings. In districts badly served by roads, agricultural rentals could not be sustained at the general level for the zone. Some of these strips of still working landscape, served only by deeply worn tracks and left aside by the high-roads, did not attract Cockney immigrants until they fell progressively within the purview of villa builders with the advent of railways and further road improvements. (See Chap. XVI).

In the story of improved communications in Surrey the Wandle valley has a special place, for its important waterside industries induced Croydon businessmen at the beginning of the 19th century to consider a tramway as a better means of conveying passengers and goods to and from London. In Cobbett's day the Wandle valley was one of the most industralised districts in England, only paralleled by the rapidly developing textile area of Lancashire and West Yorkshire. James Malcolm, who considered the little river as the hardest worked in the

74

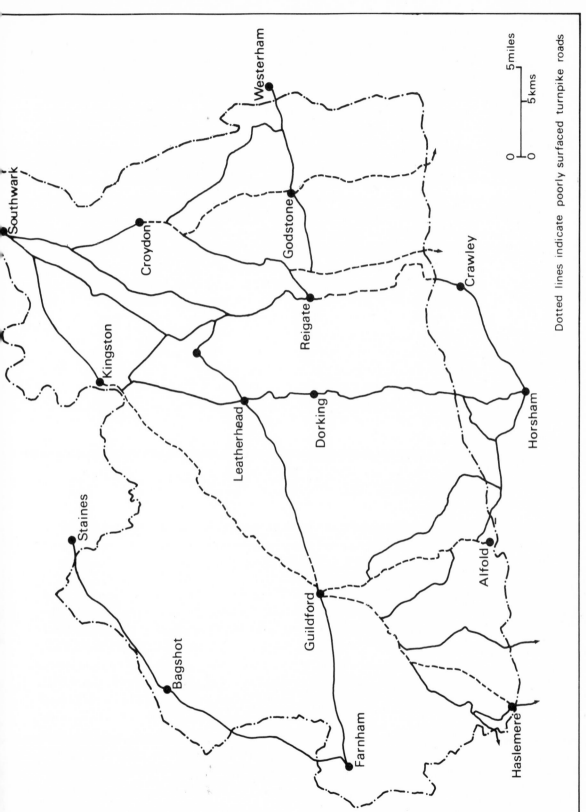

Map 8. Turnpike roads in Surrey. Information as to the condition of the surface is based on James Malcolm, *A Compendium of Modern Husbandry* (1805), vol. III, pp. 311-23.

Dotted lines indicate poorly surfaced turnpike roads

Westerham

Godstone

Croydon

Southwark

Reigate

Crawley

Kingston

Leatherhead

Dorking

Horsham

Staines

Alfold

Bagshot

Guildford

Farnham

Haslemere

0   5miles

0   5kms

world enumerated in his *Compendium* 39 industrial premises on a nine-mile stretch of the river in 1805, including 16 calico printing and bleaching works, 9 flour mills (including exceptionally large premises working several pairs of stones), 5 snuff mills, 4 oil-seed crushing mills, and a paper mill, saw mill, copper refinery, an iron works, and a brewery. For all this industrial development the great market of London was, of course, responsible. Many of the water-mills were still standing in the early years of this century. The water cornmills were tending to become ever larger units by the device of building additional water wheels of larger dimensions supplied by re-circulating water between the wheels. Shortly before 1826, for example, Home Pitt Mill at Wandsworth was adapted from a two-wheel mill working eight pairs of 'French' stones to a three-wheel mill working 11 pairs.

In 1802 the Grand Surrey Iron Railway was built from a wharf at the confluence of the Wandle and Thames at Wandsworth. Despite its grand title, this was really a short horse-drawn tramway, but it is noteworthy as the very first publicly-owned conveyance in England. In 1810 it was extended over the Downs to Bletchingley to serve the Chalk quarries and Fuller's Earth pits at Merstham and Nutfield. A little older than the tramway was a branch of the Grand Surrey Canal cut from New Cross where it joined the main canal. This was designed by Rennie in 1800 and drew water from the Thames by pumping. The canal never prospered and in 1834 the newly-formed London to Croydon Railway bought it up and laid a railway track along its bed from London Bridge. This ultimately became a branch of the London-Brighton railway.

Yet another new form of transport in Surrey was the Wey and Arun Junction Canal, now a derelict waterway. By an Act of Parliament in 1651, locks were built on the river Wey from the confluence of the Thames to Guildford and navigation was extended to Godalming in the late 18th century. The Arun Navigation was also extended to Wisborough Green. The Wey and Arun Canal, opened in 1816, was the connecting link between these canal systems, so providing an inland route between London and Portsmouth, via the Chichester Canal. The canal left the Wey at Stonebridge Wharf, Shalford, and rose by seven locks to Cranleigh, the summit level, and thence passed through a cutting at Alfold before rapidly descending by 16 locks to Loxwood en route to Newbridge, where it joined the Arun Navigation. The person most identified with the canal was George O'Brien Wyndham, the third Earl of Egremont (1751-1837), who during his long and influential life at Petworth espoused the cause of, and committed his large fortune to, agricultural improvement. The canal was never a commercial success, and after 55 years of desultory activity it was closed down. Only a few fragments of masonry or of old timbers now mark the site of the locks.

A decorative chimney crane (after Gertrude Jekyll)

76

XII *William Cobbett's Surrey (1780-1840)*

Few have looked as long and closely at the landscape of southern England and evoked its spirit so vividly in prose as William Cobbett, who was born in 1762 at Farnham and who died, after repeated travel and adventure, in 1835 at Normandy farm in Ash, only a few miles from his birthplace. Throughout a lifetime of pugnacious political writing he clung with fanatical devotion to the countryside and way of life of old Surrey which to him were the embodiment of all the traditions and virtues which he cherished as most truly English. From his pen, and especially the hurriedly-written, spontaneous, reports he published in *Rural Rides*, we can still capture an extraordinarily fresh and intimate sense of the Surrey scene in the 1820s, all the more because in his quest for first-hand knowledge, Cobbett avoided turnpikes and happily took to the byways.

Elizabethan window, Bramley

Amongst Cobbett's most vivid picturesque figures in *Rural Rides* are the 'clay and coppice' people inhabiting the Surrey Weald. In this poor and slow-changing countryside the self-supporting peasant was still living close to the soil with his bakehouse, brewhouse, pig-sty and rabbit warren. The cheerful, hard-working and comparatively well-off Wealden peasant symbolised his idea of the perfect English countryman. Strong as the soil he worked upon, he still formed part of a recognisable community, all but inaccessible to strangers, still holding his own in the self-sufficiency which was for generations in the Weald a condition of survival. His very dress proclaimed his battle with the soil.

As 'God has made the back to the burthen', so the clay and coppice people make the dress to the stubs and bushes. Under the sole of the shoe is *iron*; from the sole six inches upwards is a high-low; then comes a pair of leather breeches; then comes a stout doublet: over this comes a smock-frock; and the wearer sets brush and stubs and thorns and mire at defiance.

As one in whom the love of home and family was singularly intense, Cobbett inevitably took pride in the old Surrey farmhouses whose doors, hearths, windows and furnishings of oak tables, oak bedsteads, oak chests of drawers and oak clothes-chests, and the very scent of the air upon them, were to him expressive of all the qualities of an admired inherited past. In their presence Cobbett felt some intangible essence lingering of an earlier, homelier, England and they so vividly recalled

Ornamental barn. Mid-nineteenth century

to him an association with generations of Surrey folk that we can almost hear the farm labourers clumping in with their loud-sounding hob-nail boots and dining cheerily at the side tables, just as they had done four centuries earlier at Thorncroft (see p. 47). All this, of course, was within Cobbett's experience, the touchstone to him of everything. In the old unaltered farmhouses Cobbett had recovered a trace of the Surrey of his childhood and nostalgia swept over him. Hence his inflexible censure for 'Jews and Jobbers', the most sinister figures in his Chamber of Horrors, who were buying up Surrey farmhouses and building and furnishing in the new-fangled style of the age. Coming into Surrey in the wake of this Cockney invasion of the Surrey countryside were *parlours,* 'aye, and with a *carpet* and *bell-push* too', mahogany chairs, sofas, fine glass, wine decanters, dinner and breakfast sets, dessert knives. Such changes were to continue long after Cobbett's death and in time were to envelop all Surrey. (See Chap. XVII.)

Cobbett made another encounter with 'Jobbers' at Croydon, in 'two entire miles of stock-jobbers' houses', and again at Reigate where the Brighton turnpike was being smoothed and levelled so that they could 'skip backward and forward on the coaches and actually carry on stock-jobbing on "Change Alley", though they reside in Brighton'. The rash of new enclosures and businessmen's houses on the heaths of Windsor Forest, the aftermath of an Enclosure Act of 1818, and the sight of a rivulet turning mills making gunpowder and bank-notes at Chilworth also reduced him to a passing mood of despair.

As early as 1825, Cobbett drew a distinction between the unselfconscious face of the traditional Surrey farming landscape and the new gentry's 'artificial' landscape spreading out of London in the wake of the turnpikes. Sarcastically he cast his exact, quick, glance over the 'improvements' which frustrated his express aim to see the country's agriculture and its working farmers and labourers. The experience of a day's journey in Surrey led him to conclude that the traditional habits and sights of rural England survived only along rutted hollowways unusable to carriages such as were around Thursley and Hascombe. Beside the great high roads from London the new gentry, who were his aversion, were 'expelling' yeomanry and sensuously rearranging landscape, activities associated in Cobbett's mind with the topsy-turvydom and trumpery created by the repulsive eruption of the Great Wen.

Cobbett's distinction between two contending forces in the Surrey landscape, the one sustaining a working landscape of traditional (often mean) farm buildings rented by round-frocked farmers, the other new designs worked upon for pleasure like a piece of stage scenery, is amply borne out by other writers, though not all, of course, would have agreed with Cobbett as to which was the baser and which the better.

One of the earliest Surrey districts to be remade was the Vale of Mickleham, pierced by the river Mole in its passage through the North Downs. Its delightful wooded landscape blends so harmoniously with the contours, and so forgotten is the care lavished upon its making, that such scenery is often wrongly regarded as 'natural' to Surrey. This is the reverse of the truth. Surrey scenery is almost entirely man-made and the most beautiful landscapes are those with a history of land-owners who have cared for them. In fact, the Vale in the mid-18th century was then a bare landscape of low-rented rabbit warren and sheepwalk which was remodelled into hanging woods, woodland walks, plantations, parks and ornamental farms after the Vale became readily accessible to London with the opening of the Epsom to Horsham turnpike in 1755. Much of the achievement is due to George Lock who bought the Norbury estate in 1774 and rebuilt Norbury Park immediately afterwards. Lock's landscape room at Norbury Park (*c.* 1775) is one of the finest examples in England of 18th-century rooms painted with continuous landscapes to create the illusion that one is not inside the room but outside, surrounded by the picturesque scenery depicted. The sides of the room open to four views. The windows on the south framed the picturesque scenery then being remade in the Vale of Mickleham. The other walls of the room were generalised paintings of the Lake District by George Barret (1728–1784). This painted room represents the high watermark in the cult of the Picturesque associated with William Gilpin, who was greatly admired by Lock and whose Western Tour began at Norbury Park (Plate 31).

Asgill House, Richmond

Soon after the building of Norbury the surrounding hills were crowded with decorative mansions overlooking parks, neat bow-fronted cottages *ornées* and thickly-wooded clums of yew and box. All these landscape 'effects' spelt death to the old rural customs, especially the exercise of common rights. An example of the changes involved is an agreement made in 1789 between the lord of the manor of Headley and his 17 copy-holders whereby the lord gave up his right to the tenant's best beast on the death of a copy-holder in return for surrender of the traditional right to cut bushes, furze and underwood on the Nower.

One of the little islands of old Surrey still holding out in the early 1800s was the village of Sanderstead which, although only four miles from Croydon, the fast-growing outpost of the Great Wen, was sufficiently remote from the Brighton road to preserve its traditional ways. Amidst attractive woodland which enveloped church, manor house and fields alike, its inhabitants were 'ignorant of the many wants which luxury excites'. They awakened, we are assured, 'with the earliest dawn and repair with cheerfulness to their several occupations . . .'.

Surrey peasants, c. 1800 (after J. M. W. Turner)

This sentimental account of the Surrey scene and Cobbett's reverence of the Surrey past for the sake of its old social values contrasts with the attitude of many Surrey farmers and agricultural labourers caught up at this time in the great stream of emigration to the United States. These saw the past as a millstone around the county's neck and yearned for new lands 'where no man dwells in his father's house and where no man thinks of dying in his birthplace'. The most famous of Surrey's emigrants was the yeoman farmer Morris Birkbeck, who left the great rambling farmstead of Wanborough in 1817 to make a new home and career for himself in the frontier district of Illinois Territory. His idealistic community of Lebanon proved a failure, but the Puttenham carpenter and other Surrey persons who accompanied him have as their monument the little American town of Wanborough. In Surrey, Birkbeck was a tenant of the Earl of Onslow: in the United States he became a landowner and maker of a new community excitingly arising in the wild in what he felt to be a freer religious and social environment. He was particularly frustrated by the very archaic survivals and attitudes that William Cobbett singled out for praise. 'The inhabitants of [Surrey] villages are for the most part the children of the former inhabitants, to be succeeded by their children, ploughing the same fields and threshing the same barns from generation to generation', wrote Birkbeck. Wanborough has changed relatively little since Birkbeck departed for Illinois. The tiny church (restored from a ruin a century ago), and the huddle of large timber barns, lead to a clipped yew hedge that Birkbeck probably tended, and a garden fronting a fine brick Queen Anne house. This is evidently merely a façade, for the date 1527 is cut into a stone above the porch, at which time it was held by Waverley Abbey. Birkbeck's emigration was a great loss to Surrey agriculture. He was Surrey's largest farmer in 1805 and possessed superior skill, knowledge, livestock, farming utensils and systems of husbandry to those of most men in the county. His fine ewes crossed with Merinos and South Downs and his new threshing machine, worked by four horses, which threshed, screened and winnowed the corn, were talked about all over the county. The latter, made by James Drabble of Godalming, is one of the earliest indications that Surrey men were seeking and finding new and ingenious ways to mechanise the more burdensome work in farming. By one of the strange coincidences of history, Birkbeck's house was again to serve in the interests of toleration and freedom in the Second World War, for it was the secret training base of men and women who were dropped by parachute to assist the Resistance in enemy-occupied Europe. A plaque commemorating their achievements and heroism is placed in the church (Plate 23).

A west Surrey rustic, c.1820 (after Gertrude Jekyll)

80

26. The High Street of Guildford preserves much of its early 19th century character. Aylward's celebrated clock has a prominent position. The decorations are in celebration of Queen Elizabeth II's Silver Jubilee.

27. Castle Street, Farnham, after an original drawing, *c.* 1816.

28. (*above*) Busbridge, near Godalming, (an early 19th century house subsequently destroyed by fire). The owner is reading 'Bell's Life in London', like many other Surrey country house owners who repeatedly sped to and from London 'as if fleeing from a crime'.

29. (*left*) Farnham still wears the air of a small country town. These cottages are heavily disguised timber-framed dwellings.

30. (*right*) The splendid marble hall of Clandon Park, the seat of the Onslows, conceived by the Venetian architect Giacomo Leoni *c.*1730. The plasterwork was by the best Italian craftsmen and the celebrated Rysbrack designed the fine chimney piece.

31. (*below*) George Barret's painted room at Norbury Park.

32. (*above*) in this picture of a Surrey drawing-room, Mrs. Allingham brilliantly catches the elegance, security and confidence of the Victorian Age.

33. (*left*) One of William Kent's pen and wash drawings for his celebrated landscape at Esher Place. This provides valuable evidence of his grouping of trees.

XIII The New Agriculture (1780-1840)

William Stevenson in his *General view of the agriculture of the county of Surrey* (1809) reported 'scarcely a vestige of improvement' in any part of the Weald at that time and that 'everything in it wears the look of inadequate capital and labour misapplied'. John Burton had earlier wrongly perceived the Weald as a 'churlish soil untamed by human art'. He completely failed to recognise the extraordinary human exertion expended on the obdurate, begrudging soils. The Wealdsman's greatest pride was to be thought a good breeder of cattle and such like matters, and he still ploughed and drew his wagons with oxen in preference to horses. Travellers, in fact, who received a triple impression of wild, overgrown hedgerows, wide, riotous shaws and thistly, poor-drained fields, condemned this as proof of thriftless farming.

Eighteenth century oxen

This poor state of Wealden agriculture began to change gradually with the turnpiking. Hitherto the Weald had been a stock-rearing province. Now with a greater accessibility to market, it was possible to grow surplus grain. It became a general practice for landlords to amalgamate the former smallholdings which then left farms of 150-200 acres with many awkwardly-sited farmhouses and with small barns scattered inefficiently over every holding. Another consequence of amalgamation was that former farmhouses were used to accommodate farm labourers. Many of them were so over-filled, as the Census Returns indicate, that problems of hygiene and sanitation must have been aggravated.

The coach traveller on the Eastbourne–Godstone road in 1820 would have noted the varying response of Surrey farmers to the greater possibilities of marketing. As he entered Surrey from the south, he would have found that the traditional rotation of fallow, wheat, beans and oats still held out on the wettest patches. Passing over Tilburstow Hill, he would have entered a district of strong but better-drained clays, which when ridged up like a vast corrugated draining board yielded good crops of turnips, barley and clover in addition to the standard Wealden crops, and little grass was visible. This was a distinct zone of 'improvement'.

On leaving Godstone on the verge of the hill country of the North Downs, the scene quickly changed to flinty, downland soils. Much of this land was devoted to sheep grazing and the thin arable soils were well adapted to clover, turnips and other new root crops, but this

81

potential was not fully utilised until 50 years later. Farms were large: one at Woodmansterne was 1,200 acres in extent. The sparseness of population impressed the traveller and so also did the small neglected churches. The parish of Woldingham contained only two or three farmhouses and a few cottages, and even as late as 1811, when the Wen was beginning its encroachment, the total number of its inhabitants was only fifty-eight. Its church consisted of one room about 30ft. long and 21ft. wide, without tower, spire, or bell. Even in Evelyn's day, it had been dilapidated, desolately standing upon its hill; its restoration was not undertaken until 1890 when Woldingham was inhabited by villa builders. The appearance of Farleigh was still almost unchanged from its 14th-century aspect as a hamlet on the estate of Merton College. Its little church had not been structurally altered since 1250. The Rev. J. Kilner, the rector in 1767, observed that it was a parish of roughly 1,000 acres, but containing only 20 families and a total population of 94, of which 18 resided at the manor house of Farleigh Court and nine at the Rectory. He also explained that only half of the arable of 700 acres was annually under corn: the remainder had to be sown to grass. Yet another of the thinly-populated parishes on the North Downs was Walton-on-the-Hill. Its church was declared to be in such a dangerous and dilapidated condition in 1818 that the Bishop of Winchester granted a faculty to rebuild the church except the chancel and part of the tower. The old church of Titsey was also pulled down in 1775 and one built in its place was superseded yet again in 1861 by the present church. The west wall of Warlingham church, rebuilt in the 17th century, was partially pulled down in the restoration of 1893–4. These details of church building convey an impression of the poverty of scantily-populated parishes until the invasion of London business people in the late 19th century.

After passing through busy Croydon, the coach traversed a rich hay and dairying belt on wet, cold clays, but ameliorated with copious London dung. At the fifth milestone from London Bridge, the farms disappeared and nurserymen, gardeners and cow-keepers were interspersed between brick-makers and the scattered residences of London business men as far as Brixton Causeway. The most delightful nursery gardens were those growing plants for the perfumer and chemists. Mitcham and Sutton were famous for lavender, peppermint, camomile, liquorice, poppy and musk-roses. Oils were distilled on the nurseries which were dependent on huge quantities of London dung. This horticulture survived in Mitcham until the early years of this century.

Something of the appearance of the Surrey farming landscape can be recaptured from contemporary manuscript estate maps. Farms in the Vale of Holmesdale were still wedded to their numerous small

Gleaners (after John Constable)

82

enclosures, little altered since the 15th century. Hoopwich Farm, comprising 116 acres of Abinger had 23 fields in 1780 and the neighbouring Paddington Manor Farm of 179 acres was divided into 25 fields at the same date. Rather exceptional were Sir John Evelyn's Paddington and Mill Farms, comprising 315 acres, which had been relaid out in a series of uniformly straight-sided, square or sub-rectangular fields of about 10 acres, each bordered by neat hedgerows and served by good drove-ways. The date of this remodelling is uncertain but at Coombe Farm the origin of several such 'model' fields on former poor ground on the flanks of the Downs escarpment can be dated to the period 1742–1772 from extant maps.

Improved sheep, eighteenth century

On Surrey estate maps of about 1740 to 1850 there is invariably marked a centrally-placed lime kiln on the wayside. Lime was applied each time acidic land lay fallow, about once in five or six years on the Weald Clay and a little less frequently on the also rather sour Upper and Lower Greensand. Until the widespread distribution of lime from the quarry kilns became practicable with the introduction of railways and improved by-ways, almost every farmer on acid soils carted lime to his own kiln. This was built of stone, 18 to 20ft. high, and shaped like a round tower. Earth was heaped around one side to provide a ramp so that the kiln could be fed from the top. The lime-burner raked with a long pole the furze or wood fire every 20 minutes or so and rested little during the three-day operation, regularly sending up flames into the darkness.

Despite some general progress since Stevenson's *Report* of 1813 observers in the 1850s were still very critical of the backward state of Surrey agriculture. James Caird in his *English agriculture in 1850-1* took as an illustration the 'undrained marshes, ill-kept roads, untrimmed hedges, rickety farm-buildings, shabby-looking cows of various breeds and dirty cottages' encountered on a walk from Gomshall railway station. He attributed most of this neglect to the pernicious custom of letting farms on yearly leases, a practice favoured by tenants who fraudulently 'worked out' a farm and received from an incoming tenant payment for 'imaginary improvements and alleged operations'. This bad system was the staple of numerous Surrey land agents and valuers whose shiny brass plates were a feature of every little town in the county. An exceptional improvement was the farming at Albury which everyone connected with the banker Henry Drummond. He enlarged his park, set out the present estate village, built two churches, a fine Romanesque for the new village and a Roman Catholic church in the park, leaving the old church a ruin. At the other extreme was the still badly farmed Weald, which Caird correctly considered could not be cultivated much longer because of need of under-drainage.

XIV Remodelling the Landscape (1760-1840)

We have already noted that the Surrey landscape was being remade in the 18th and the early 19th centuries. Throughout England in this period country estates were remodelled in the informal naturalistic manner of William Kent, 'Capability' Brown and Humphry Repton. The ambition of such creators of designed landscape was to reproduce in the English countryside the romantic kind of scenery around Rome and Tivoli, idealised on the canvases of Claude Lorrain and Nicholas Poussin. The best known of its most brilliantly creative works are the rich grass parks characteristic of the large estate. Another artistic response was the ornamental farm (*ferme ornée*) of the gentleman farmer, conceived on the principle of combining the two seemingly opposites of beauty and use, a cheaper and more practical design than a park and suitable for a small estate. Yet another style in this new approach to landscape art was the 'forest' or 'savage garden' where the principal effects were gained not by deliberately reducing middle distances with grass as in parks, but by planting up trees in 'wild' situations. Moreover, many country landowners advanced the visual arts by laying-out not parks alone but by creating wider landscapes where the park was the focal point from which their aesthetic concern was irradiated over the estate at large.

Chimneys at Albury estate village, early nineteenth century imitations of Jacobean workmanship

The face of Surrey bears the distinguishing marks of this scenery contrived by successive generations. The proximity of Surrey to London, and its greater accessibility on account of the turnpikes was a fundamental cause of its popularity amongst potential adopters of new designs. Another stimulus was the existing garden-like quality of much of its scenery. Surrey has always offered to the observer the continual succession of little landscapes of great beauty 'compart-mented into small scenes furnished with belfried church towers, half-timbered thatch cottages, rutted lanes, rookeried elms, lich gates and stiles', which has long been considered the ideal English scenery. The goal of Hanoverian royalty and courtiers and the newly-rich in the first half of the 18th century was the Thames riverside west of London. The valley between Windsor and Chiswick became a source region of innovation in landscape. An astonishingly creative *forte* was established on the banks of the Thames in the 1740s: Lord Burlington at Chiswick, an original mind behind English Palladianism; Horace Walpole, re-creating in the Gothic style at Strawberry Hill;

Hon. Charles Hamilton of Pains Hill, Cobham, the originator of the 'alpine' or 'savage' garden; Philip Southcote of Woburn Farm, near Chertsey, and others, experimenting with the *ferme ornée*; William Kent, artist and landscapist working at Esher Place and Claremont—their activity spans little more than a single generation. The district was one of the primary sources of many new and influential ideas on English landscape gardening which were eventually diffused over the whole of Britain and also to the continent as the 'English garden'. When William Gilpin, the celebrated writer on the 'Picturesque' and his brother, the artist Sawrey Gilpin, rowed down the Thames between Windsor and London in 1746, the Thameside west of London was even then no longer truly rural. The simplicity of the former natural meadows had gone and every foot of land on both the Surrey and Middlesex banks of the river Thames displayed 'an air of high improvement, expense and splendour'. Gilt barges, pleasure boats, and new bridges heralded handsome houses crowding everywhere on the sight. Henrietta Pye's journey in 1760 along the great thoroughfare of the Thames in the vicinity of Richmond and Twickenham led to the discovery of a string of luxury villas which made the whole river a continuous garden or a continuous town, according to whether you appreciated the more the landscaping, as did Henrietta Pye, or the social life, which was Walpole's preference.

Leatherhead Church from the Rev. James Dallaway's vicarage, c. 1821

Amongst the earliest of the Surrey works of art were the influential landscapes of Esher and Claremont owned by the Whig leader, the Duke of Newcastle, and his brother, Lord Pelham, respectively. Of the former place, only Waynflete's 15th-century tower survives and it is now a modern housing estate, but William Kent's pen-and-wash sketch (Plate 33) is of great historic value in recording the evolution of 18th-century tree clump planting. Claremont bears the marks of four famous designers: Vanbrugh, who built the original house and laid out formal gardens within massive bailey-like walled defences and a fort-like belvedere tower; Bridgeman, who converted the walled parterre into a ha-ha (1715–1726), but leaving traces of Vanbrugh's work which are traceable to this day; Kent (1738), who designed the rectangular lake, amphitheatre, cascade, and arranged trees in informal groups; and 'Capability' Brown, who extended the park and added more water features. The mansion, occupied for a time by Clive of India, has been demolished, but the landscaped gardens are owned by the National Trust who have undertaken much restoration, tree surgery and replanting, so revealing to its full effect this important 18th-century landscape garden which was a genesis of informal landscape in England.

One of the first and most celebrated of Surrey's new garden landscapes was that laid out in the 1740s and 1750s over some

Gothic temple, Pains Hill, Cobham

400 acres by the Hon. Charles Hamilton at Pains Hill, Cobham. Much of the character of Hamilton's art still survives, notably its fine trees for which the estate is now famed. As Price explained in *An Essay on the Picturesque* (1794), Hamilton was one of the first to study the paintings of Old Masters such as Claude Lorrain and Nicholas Poussin for the express purpose of 'improving' real landscape. The great merit of Hamilton as an amateur landscape designer was his ability to enhance the latent natural beauties of a site. 'He has really made a fine place out of a most cursed hill'. wrote Horace Walpole in 1748. The setting of Painshill was originally farmland spreading out within a peninsula of land bounded by meanders of the river Mole undercutting the sand into steep bluffs. Hamilton planted up the river cliffs in pine (now largely colonised by actively regenerating beech) in reminiscence of paintings by Poussin (Plate 19).

A cheaper and more practical precept of design in landscape which contributed to the re-facing of Surrey was the *ferme ornée* (ornamental or villa farm) which was not so much a business as an essay in the Picturesque. In the *ferme ornée* the farm offices were often joined to the house and the grounds were laid out with a view to utility as well as beauty.

On the authority of George Mason and Horace Walpole, it was Philip Southcote (the purchaser of Woburn Farm, near Chertsey, in 1735) who was the originator of the *ferme ornée,* but this claim does not appear to be substantiated by the evidence now being gathered by present students of landscape gardening. Stephen Switzer, who used the term 'ornamental farm' before Southcote bought Woburn Farm, noted in 1733 the 'farm-like way of gardening in the manner of a Roman villa which had been practised in France for some time'. In 1742 Switzer published a plan of a *ferme ornée* laid out by Lord Bathurst at Riskins, near Colnbrook, Middlesex, and he also mentions ornamental farms at Abbs Court (Molesey) and Dawley (Harmondsworth, Middlesex). The plan of Riskins, of which Switzer was probably the designer in the 1720s, was on the rigidly-patterned design of the French geometrical school of landscaping and its inspiration was the Roman farm-*villa rustica*. Switzer's generation was so predisposed towards the classical theme that it became part of the mind of England, and Alexander Pope's circle (which included Cotterell of Abbs Court as well as Lord Bolingbroke of Dawley and Lord Bathurst who owned Riskins and Cirencester Park) were especially favourable to the more practical forms of estate management than the recent ornamental excesses of the 17th-century.

It was Philip Southcote's achievement to change completely the visual relationship of garden and farmland by adopting as his basic

86

principle Addison's *Spectator* pronouncement (1712) that tree planting and other embellishments should be extended into fields and meadows 'so that a man might make a pretty landskip of his own possessions'. Little now survives recognisably of his work at Woburn Farm, near Chertsey, but from Thomas Whateley's description in *Observations on Modern Gardening* we can make a reconstruction. The ornamental farm contained 150 acres, of which 35 were 'adorned to the highest degree', the remainder being a working farm. Southcote applied Addison's principle chiefly by making a tree-lined gravel walk around the boundary of his farm, which afforded framed views both inwards and outwards of other country homes, Gothic buildings and temples. His tree-lined boundary belt very probably greatly influenced 'Capability' Brown, who used the feature in his re-designed parks.

The willow, Rev. James Dallaway's garden, Leatherhead, c.1821

In the second half of the 18th century, the rather elaborate ornamentation of Southcote gave way to a simpler and more obviously useful type of ornamented farm. Thomas Ruggles, an able Surrey and Suffolk farmer, devoted much attention to this topic in the 1780s. He advocated a turreted ornamental farmhouse surrounded by woodland opened up by wide rides to give prospects of near farm cottages and well-bred livestock. He advised the repair of old hedges with whitethorn, crab, holly, sweet briar, and honeysuckle, and suggested that single trees planted out of the way of the plough in the 'short lands' of the fields should include Scots pine, larch, silver fir, and Weymouth pine. He recommended trees natural to watersides—aspen, white poplar, Carolina pine and Lombardy poplar to improve meadows and brooks. None of this 'picturesque planting', as Ruggles termed it, was considered to compromise 'the absolute necessity of an attention to good cultivation'. It is this vision of a new Surrey landscape based on the free planting of trees, adopted by so many past Surrey landowners, that has imparted such a widespread glory to the county.

An example of Ruggles' model of a *ferme ornée* was Thorncroft in the Vale of Mickleham. The mansion, built in 1766 on an ornamented estate of 121 acres, was laid out in regular 14–16 acre fields, well planted up with trees and luxurious hedgerows. Something of its former appearance is still recognisable in the landscape, but its former atmosphere is perhaps even more preserved in the exquisite and ingenious map of F. T. Young (1822), itself a minor work of art. This depicts in perspective view the variegated autumn foliage of its hedges, spiked with poplar and conifers, and tree-shrouded farm buildings reflected in the waters of the river Mole. Jane Austen brilliantly captures the essence of this re-modelled landscape and of its self-satisfied makers at 'Highbury' (Leatherhead) in *Emma* (1816).

XV The Surrey Towns

Surrey shares with its neighbouring counties an inheritance of old towns built to a scale appropriate to its landscape and filled with gracefully proportioned houses so carefully preserved that they have retained much of their old identity and character. Indeed, most of the old Surrey towns possess the quality which Thomas Sharp in *English Panorama* has said: 'We in England once showed a natural genius—the genius of creating towns that nearly always have had pleasantness and seemliness; that often have quite remarkable beauty; that always have maintained a comfortable human scale'. Two of the towns sited in the classic gaps through the Chalk escarpment of the North Downs— Farnham and Guildford—have townscapes of an architectural quality that places them amongst the finest English country towns and they are matched by the unspoilt parts of Richmond-upon-Thames, a town of quite a different origin, and by the lesser towns of Godalming and Haslemere. In few parts of England is it still possible to savour so much of Georgian beauty and refinement. These townscapes vividly demonstrate the cleavage between Victorian and the earlier Surrey. It is impossible to explain why these towns are such remarkably unspoilt expressions of the pre-railway age without exploring their origins and development, and also of such rivals as Redhill, Hindhead and Woking, new towns constructed with the coming of the railways, when the pattern of human existence in Surrey was changing so rapidly. The lack of 19th-century industrial development in Surrey also needs to be borne in mind.

Seventeenth-century cottage facade

Before the Census Returns beginning in 1801 there is little in the way of accurate statistics of the urban population, but a reasonably satisfactory ranking of Surrey towns can be based on the assessments for Hearth Tax in the 1660s which provide information as to the number of houses, and hence, in some measure, of population. On this basis Guildford and Kingston-upon-Thames were in the first rank of Surrey's market towns, each comprising about 500 houses. Farnham, with about 300 dwellings, came next in size. Croydon, Godalming and Reigate had an intermediate position in the county with about 160–180 houses each. Epsom, Dorking and Leatherhead were small towns in the class of only 100–120 houses, whilst Haslemere with about 80 houses was really only an urban village, although sending two members to the unreformed Parliament. These market towns were all eclipsed in size by the large concentrations of population on the Surrey banks of the Thames near London. Bermondsey in the 1660s, for example, consisted of 800 densely-packed dwellings, many occupied by people so poor that they were exempted from taxation.

Although **Epsom** had long been supplanted as a spa by the late 18th century and was then in competition with the new sea-bathing places, it continued to thrive as a resort for London merchants and gentry intent on racing and hunting. Numerous country seats existed on the fringes of the town, one of which, Ashtead, is a particularly rewarding place to visit. **Dorking** gained in some respects from the building of the London to Brighton turnpike, but lost in others. The London gentry 'discovered' the beauty of its local scenery and in summer took up residence in the town, dining on the freshwater fish and poultry for which the town had long been renowned. Seafish was conveyed to these pampered guests by means of fast carriages from Brighton and Worthing. Although residentially the town prospered, its corn and cattle markets declined in favour of Horsham, also on the London to Brighton turnpike, and better placed for the collection of Low Weald produce. This commercial setback probably explains the report of its 'old, ill-built and badly paved' appearance by a writer in the *Gentleman's Magazine* in 1787. Unrejuvenated by the railway until the late 19th century (Dorking had no direct connection with London until 1867) the decayed old town was then largely rebuilt by the generation witnessing the rise of Woodyer's splendid new parish church (1868–77), dominating the wide streets and setting the theme for the entire town.

Early nineteenth century coachman

Leatherhead is one of many English places provided with the essentials of a medieval town, in this case, four streets meeting in a market-place at the cross-roads, which nevertheless failed to grow beyond the scale of a village until modern times. One of the main reasons for Leatherhead's past smallness was the difficulty of road communication through the Mole valley in winter, alluded to on page 79. Not until the speeding up of the tempo of human communication in the coaching era did Leatherhead become a 'gap' town commanding a major route to the coast through the Vale of Mickleham. In 1821, the Rev. James Dallaway, remarked that the village 'is losing its primary character and converting itself by a multiplication of inconsiderable houses into an appendage of the enormous London . . .'. So much of Leatherhead bore the marks of obsolescence in the newcomers' eyes that even by Dallaway's day almost all the old buildings had been demolished.

Farnham is a beautiful little town which has kept much of its identity as an old market and coaching town, living on the products of its local countryside and keeping busy its corn and hop merchants,

Farnham hop growing

89

*Farnham corn market
(after Nigel Temple)*

drovers and wheelwrights. Its history in the 18th century was not one of decline, as at Dorking, but of rising prosperity, and this is reflected in its different townscape which has been preserved by a remarkable exercise in voluntary effort. We can still enjoy the visual delight of a Georgian townscape which Christopher Hussey and Nigel Temple have described as the best in England. Farnham is a typical example of a town organically evolving through time within a country setting. The roofs of medieval Farnham covered barns and little farmsteads along its single street below the Bishop of Winchester's castle commanding the easiest route between Southampton and London. From early times a cloth town, in the 17th century it came into prominence as a great corn market, the largest in southern England during the period when coastal shipping was hindered by almost continuous warfare in the English Channel. By the 1720s, as Defoe reports, the corn trade had fallen away with the competition of Chichester and the revived seaborne route to London, but the culture of hops, begun at Farnham at the end of the 16th century, came to provide most of the wealth of the town. Hops were grown on the former common fields lying on the narrow strip, only a few hundred yards wide, marked by the Upper Greensand outcrop. Not until the 1860s did Farnham expand and disperse the hop growers along the whole length of this exposure at the foot of the Hog's Back. Hops became the *raison d'être* of Farnham to the extent that hop kilns were built in its streets, business people shut up their shops for a week at drying time, and the quick-set hedges and belts of trees erected to shelter the hops from the wind gave added beauty to its countryside. The hops were mainly marketed at Weyhill in Hampshire and were consumed by brewers from the West Country and the Midlands. Those who made the remarkable collection of little and middling buildings in present-day Farnham were mainly corn and hop merchants. The splendid façades of their warm brick, classically door-cased houses, in Castle Street and the many little yards attached to the smaller houses in East and West Streets, constitute one of the most distinguished townscapes in Surrey (Plates 25, 27 and 29).

We have already traced the history of **Guildford** to the mid-16th century. The town by then had greatly declined from its medieval importance. John Speed remarked in 1611 that 'it had been far greater than now it is when the palace of our English kings was therein set'. A further cause of impoverishment was the decline of the woollen industry which led George Abbot, Archbishop of Canterbury and native of Guildford, to endow in 1619 the Hospital of the Blessed Trinity to alleviate the town's distress. This fine brick building, reminiscent of an early Tudor gatehouse, still survives with little alteration. A further vivid reminder of Guildford's decline is the

90

beautifully-made plan of the town by Matthew Richardson in 1739, depicting the little town still bounded by its medieval defences. Little change had probably occurred in the cramped nature of the town's site for over 500 years.

In the second half of the 17th century, however, there are signs of a rejuvenation at Guildford. The outstanding event was the construction of the river Wey Navigation, opened in 1653 on the initiative of Sir Richard Weston on Sutton Place, who brought from Holland the idea of artificially controlling water in a working river by locks. One of the citizens of Guildford most closely connected with this scheme was Richard Scotcher. He was an important dyer and clothier with a 'pumpe' in Castle Street (probably a device for pumping water from an artesian well). He is one of the few clothiers once making the excellent Guildford blue cloth whose names have come down to us. Scotcher himself was driven into bankruptcy by the mismanaged Wey Navigation but it brought lasting benefit to Guildford as a means of cheap and effective transport of bulk goods such as grain, timber and building materials. The greatest source of trouble to the owners of the Wey Navigation were the millers along the river. For nearly two centuries it was their habit to draw off so much water into their mill ponds that some grain barges could not get through the locks and owners were obliged to have corn ground at their mills. A great treadmill crane on Guildford Wharf, a memento of this long era of water transport, has been preserved and by the generosity of Harry W. Stevens, the last representative of Guildford's long line of watermen, the banks of the river Wey have been taken into the custody of the National Trust. A further sign of growing prosperity in Guildford in the late 17th century was the rebuilding of the Guildhall in the High Street in 1683. To this is still affixed John Aylward's celebrated clock, provided with a fine new case when the Guildhall was altered, but in fact probably more than a century older. It was given to the Elizabethan town by Aylward who was first refused permission by the Gild Merchant to set up in business in the town as a clockmaker because he was a 'foreigner' (Plate 26).

With the final decay of its cloth industry at the beginning of the 18th century, Guildford increasingly relied for prosperity upon its growing coaching trade to Brighton, Portsmouth and Southampton. Several of its old inns still retain their rambling yards and stabling, a legacy of their former function as posting houses. Although modern manufacturing industry is now extensive at Guildford the outward appearance of the High Street and its adjacent streets is very little changed from what Matthew Richardson saw in 1739. 'The gables, bay windows, Tudor chimneys, timber and plaster walls, sundials and

Seventeenth century Guild Hall, Guildford, with John Aylward's celebrated Eliabethan clock

John Aylward's clock are all there', permeating the present townscape. Unhappily, large department stores now overpower the small domestic scale of the older buildings at Guildford, but in few parts of the London Region does one have a greater sense of a vigorous, living town, a growing organism, which has chosen to regard the past not as an encumbrance, but as an enrichment of the present and an inspiration for the future (Plate 48).

Richmond-upon-Thames, anciently named Shene from the beauty of its green hill reflected in the shining river, and for long a minor part of the royal manor of Kingston, first came into repute with its choice as a residence by the Plantagenet kings. With the rebuilding of the palace on a magnificent scale around two main courtyards by Henry VIII, who renamed the place Richmond after his birthplace and earldom in Yorkshire, Richmond became increasingly a centre of fashion and pleasure during the Tudor dynasty. A delightful painting in the style of the Flemish School of *c.* 1629 is evidence that Richmond still retained all the characteristics of a rural village. A century later, as is disclosed in the engraving of 'The Prospect of Richmond' (1726) by H. Overton and J. Hook, Richmond then possessed more of an urban atmosphere, but the Georgians who created Richmond did not intend to make a town but a country retreat and consequently Richmond has none of the noble planning of Bath or Brighton, no wide streets, stately crescents and few of the bow windows and hooded balconies we normally associate with the Regency. Instead Richmond became a fashionable playground for frustrated urban Georgians who left their town houses in Mayfair and Leicester Square at the week-end and during the summer. Horace Walpole's correspondence throws much light on this social process that still gives a special air to Richmond and which underlines the spread of Richmond's buildings discoverable on one of John Rocque's maps. Under 1789 he writes: 'Richmond is the first request this summer. Mrs. Bouverie is settled there with a large court. The Sheridans are there, too, and the Bunbury's'. Forty years earlier he had remarked upon the new fashion of leaving London at the week-end. 'As I passed over the Green I saw Lord Bath, Lord Lonsdale and half-dozen more of the White's Club . . . come to Richmond every Saturday and Sunday to play at whist . . . [it is now] a fashion to go out of town at the end of the week . . .'. (Plates 16 and 17).

It was in the Georgian period that Richmond enjoyed its greatest fame as a resort. Its Green, its Park (imparked by Charles I in 1637), its unrivalled riverside scenery observable from Richmond Hill, and its accessibility, made it a perfect resort for Londoners. It also enjoyed the consistent and enthusiastic patronage of Hanoverian royalty.

Richmond Palace, 1562 (after Anthonis van den Wyngaerde)

92

Society flocked in its wake and this was a decisive factor in the accelerated building during the later 18th century. The eldest son of George I resided at Richmond Lodge, a Palladian house formerly standing in the grounds of the Old Deer Park. On his succession to the throne as George II, White Lodge in Richmond Park was built for him as a hunting lodge and banquetting hall. His son, Frederick Prince of Wales, remodelled the White House at Kew and it was at this house, now demolished, that George III spent summer away from the formalities of Windsor. His children were provided with houses on or near Kew Green and one, the Duke of Clarence (later King William IV) became one of the most highly regarded of Richmond's patrons. The Prince Regent, who lavished all his affection on Brighton, was the sole member of George III's large family who was not closely identified with Richmond.

The pagoda, Kew by Sir William Chambers, 1761-2

Under this royal patronage Richmond became a metropolitan pleasure adjunct, bearing something of the kind of relationship that Versailles did to the 18th-century Paris. Repeated balls, masquerades, regattas and firework displays, all on a magnificent scale, were the main events of the summer season. Visitors and residents ambled around Richmond Park in their chaises; promenaded on the Green, a special ornament of the town to this day, and originally the 'pleasance' to the Tudor palace turned to good account as a 'village green'; or sauntered along the riverside and contemplated the most famous view in England, a gift to the Claudian artist. 'Richmond', wrote Mary Russell Mitford, 'is Nature in a Court dress . . . gay, happy and elegant as one of Charles the Second's beauties and with as little to remind one of the penalty of labour, or poverty, or grief, or crime'. Not surprisingly, men distinguished in the arts, especially in music, drama, literature and painting, resided at Richmond to be with their wealthy patrons. They included James Thompson, author of *The Seasons,* the most unqualified tribute to the Thames landscape, and the tragedian, Edmund Kean, both buried in the parish church. Others included Thomas Gainsborough, the artist, buried at Kew, David Garrick, Richard Sheridan and Sir Joshua Reynolds, the first president of the Royal Academy, whose country house on Richmond Hill was designed by the architect, Sir William Chambers, also the designer of the Pagoda, Orangery and temples erected in the royal grounds of the White House, Kew, and still existing in the present Royal Botanical Gardens. The painting entitled 'Richmond Hill on the Prince Regent's birthday, 1819', by J. M. W. Turner, R.A. (himself a local resident) is probably the best visible expression of the gaiety and brilliance of the affluent society that gathered on the banks of the river Thames to enjoy life in the manner of the gay folk in one of Watteau's pictures.

93

XVI   The Land of Heart's Desire (1840 - 1918)

The Hallams, Shamley Green, by Richard Norman Shaw

To the Victorian businessman's mind, Surrey was paradisal, the land of his dreams, a great beckoning landscape of verdant charm to which he irresistibly surrendered. Over the length and breadth of Surrey horse-drawn carriages daily came out of trim lodge gates bearing members of the business community towards the nearest railway station to the accompaniment of the distant whistle of a London-bound train. Each evening these excellent men of business 'their names good upon 'Change for anything they chose to put their hand to' returned from their counting house under the soot-laden pall of London leaving only a brass plate to tell the Cockney passer-by where their money was made. With very few exceptions the old great families of Surrey became extinct and their estates passed into the hands of bankers, stockbrokers and distillers.

Country houses, in fact, became an established part of the life of the Victorian middle-class and changed the face of Surrey in a single generation. To select a fair and high locality, not too far away from London, and to make there a modish place where his family could enjoy fresh air and such country luxuries as fresh milk and other farm produce, was the over-riding ambition of the successful. London was perceived as so pre-eminently a city *within* doors that only country houses as Victorians knew them were seen to fulfil the requirements for health, recreation and repose. The ownership of land also conferred social and political prestige. It furthermore offered a means of gratifying the aim of the rising Victorian middle class to improve on an inheritance and hand it on for future enlargement. The wealthy Victorian wanted to be remembered not only for being a successful person, but also for contributing to charity and for building something for the community. Many Victorian landowners took this role so seriously that they considered landownership almost a sacred trust involving responsibility to tenants and staff, as well as providing pleasure.

It is easy in Surrey to detect the unmistakeable character of former large landed estates. From afar, clumps of conifer such as Calabrian pine, Norwegian spruce and noble fir are reminders of the vanished way of life as well as making a major contribution to the art of landscape. Near at hand winding, laurel-girt, public roads conceal with the

94

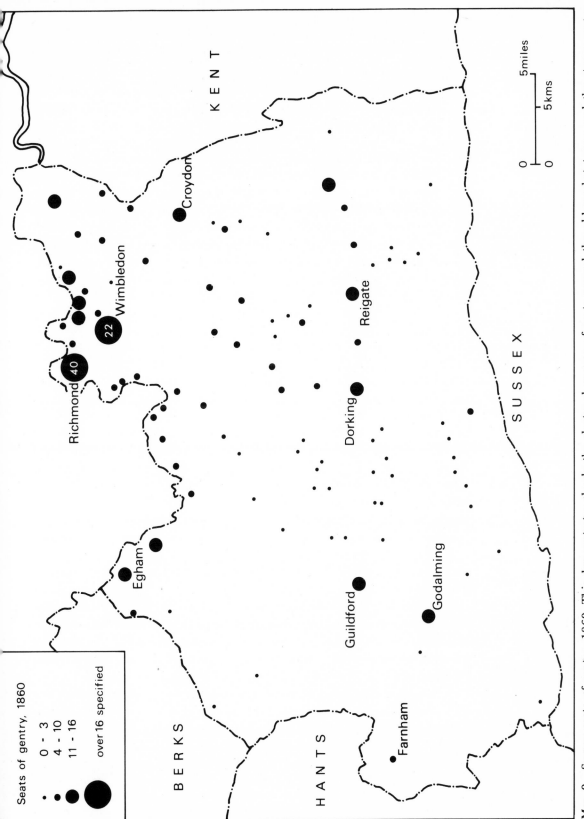

Map 9. Surrey seats of gentry, 1860. This demonstrates clearly the clustered groups of seats around the old market towns and the strong metropolitan focus before the wider diffusions of the Railway Age.

decorum of a drive wide sweeps of once raked and watered gravel leading to red-gabled villas. Thicker hedgerows, formerly well-kept luxuriant woodland, neat, 'model' fields and ornamental farm buildings are also characteristics. In these once trim villa gardens, heavy with the scent of pines, one inevitably recalls the Betjemanite allusion to the twang of the tennis racket heard behind prunus, almost symbolic of Victorian Surrey in many minds. In fact, one Surrey was blotting out another in the late 19th century, and there was little continuity between the new and the old. The persistence of rural life with the same recognisable structure over a thousand years was fast breaking up. Self-made businessmen brought some of the ways of Birmingham brass foundries and Yorkshire woollen mills with them and were sometimes impatient of a past which did not seem to belong to them. Inevitably the old Surrey labourers expressed some dissatisfaction with their new employers. 'In the old days, although their wages were less, there were privileges and "pickings" to be got from the old gentry . . . which they miss now that their lands and the land they till are owned by new men of capital who do not dress or walk like the traditional country gentlemen' (Map 9, p. 95; Plates 28, 32, 36).

Furthermore, the spread of unpleasantly obtrusive villas in formerly undiscovered parts of Surrey, representing the most serious assault on the face of the county up to that time, was agonising to those acutely appreciative of its earlier wildness and solitude. Meredith became increasingly concerned in the 1890s at the 'hectoring of lovely country by hideous villas' and a visit by William Morris to the Wealden oak-country at Witley a little earlier had left him surprised at its being 'amazingly free from anything Cockney-based', though the growing villadom of urban interlopers of Hindhead repelled him. Roger Fry, the leading art critic, who built a villa near Guildford, half-apologised to visitors for a countryside spotted with so many 'gentlemanly residences'. An interesting sidelight on the evaluation of house sites by the much less affluent is afforded by Samuel Palmer's restless quest for a small house in Surrey.

The growing demand for land by speculative builders in Surrey pushed up land prices and many cottages lost their traditional way of life when commons were enclosed and sold off by lords of manors in convenient building lots for purchase. Land was divided into house-lots and sold, sub-divided and sold again, and often 'boomed' and re-sold once more. 'In the Hands of the Builders' was a familiar sign in the countryside. The uncontrolled spread of building in the county (which broadly went up and down with the annual figures of English coal production) brought a crisis the worst of its kind in

Georgian chair, Guildford England.

34. Reigate, early 19th century.

35. Pugin's medieval creation at Oxenford Grange, Elstead, near Farnham.

36. (*above*) Braboeuf House, near Guildford, from
an original early 19th-century drawing. A typical
ferme ornée of the period.

37. (*left*) Surrey Lane, Long Ditton, from an early
19th-century drawing.

38. (*above*) *Contemplation* by John Linnell. The discovery of the Surrey 'wildscape' by artists reflects the renewed interest in woodland which is also attributable to William Robinson's Wild Gardens.

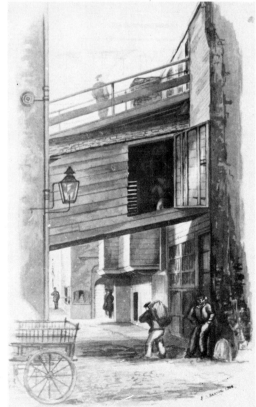

39. (*right*) Montague Close, Southwark, mid 19th century.

40. Guildford, High Street

The private homes of the wealthy in this 'highly favoured county' were by 1900 turning Surrey into a mere ravelled fringe of ever outwardly developing London. Public concern was expressed for the North Down ridge. 'We have now reached a stage', said *The Spectator* in 1912, one of the leading organs of enlightened opinion, 'when the further placing of houses along the ridge can only spoil and disfigure the ridge as a whole . . .'. Along this range of hills were the residence of persons who had amassed wealth from ships, tea, pottery, iron, law, banking, coal, and 'contracting'. An incalculable debt is owed to public-spirited people who responded to *The Spectator's* appeal for money to buy Colley Hill, near Reigate, which came on to the building market. This lovely hill, offering vistas of the whole Weald, was purchased for £7,700 by public subscription in 1912 and taken into the management of the National Trust. Earlier *The Spectator* had successfully appealed for money to purchase farmland in the Wandle Valley. The Great War and the ensuing depression soon afterwards put the speculative builder temporarily out of business.

A suburban house, small by late Victorian standards

The term *ferme ornée* gradually dropped out of use in the early 19th century and late Victorian gentry spoke of a 'pleasure farm' when they wished to denominate an agricultural estate largely turned over to ornament and leisure. The change in name coincided with a change in taste. The *ferme ornée* was generally a newly-built and often rather whimsical residence, verandahed and bedecked with french windows and other prettiness to attract the eye. The 'pleasure farm' symbolises the pronounced swing of taste to the eclectic and the revivalist forms of architecture. Its dwelling was typically a renovated half-timbered or stone-built yeoman's farmstead or small existing manor house. Such property came cheaply on the market in the last quarter of the 19th century as the prices for heavy land of mediocre quality tumbled with the increasing import of corn from overseas. With the growth of trans-Wealden railways between London and the coast, 'pleasure farms' for sporting purposes became characteristic of the Surrey Weald, a landscape so gentle as to be undistinguished except for trees packed close like a hedge. Such stretches of low country left most people comparatively unresponsive to its quiet beauty and they did not afford the prospects deemed essential for the perfect villa landscape, so that outwardly the traditional Surrey landscape has survived more than elsewhere. John Ruskin published in *Fors Clavigera* an account of the process which transformed a Surrey working countryside into a 'cocktail belt' with all its resultant social upheaval. A Cranleigh resident reported in 1887 that some years previously 'some manufacturers and others who had made large fortunes in "trade" came to settle in that part of Surrey and bought

97

Early Georgian chair,
Guildford

farms, or hired them for much higher rents than normal'. This led to a rise in land rents for the entire district, putting farmers in great difficulty. The new masters also paid higher wages than the old and 'not knowing what was a fair day's work permitted less and less . . .'. The migrants soon had a new house built about the farm, or were engaged in renovating and enlarging the old, and then induced the parish to make up the green lanes into hard roads at great expense and the consequent increase in the parish rates was another nail in the farmer's coffin.

Even by 1914 some of the special charm of Surrey county roads had been destroyed by the tree-lopping and grubbing of roadside hedges and trees in the interests of motorists and the insistent nearness of London became apparent to travellers through large wooden advertisement hoardings placed in fields alongside roads and railways. The ubiquitous use of corrugated iron and a widespread litter problem were also new difficulties in the management of the Surrey environment which had become evident before the First World War. Yet a mile or two from the chief roads and railways one could still plunge into tracts of country which were not only singularly picturesque, but very thinly peopled. It was at this time of fast change that surveys and inventories were first made of Surrey's historical heritage. A remarkably early and active body were the amateur photographers who founded the Photographic Survey and Record of Surrey in 1902, which by 1911 had yielded a collection of 5,000 prints. The Photographic Survey was continued between the wars and the valuable collection of prints is preserved at Croydon Public Library. Unfortunately, the Record insufficiently covered the old farmhouses, inns and landscape features which have now disappeared forever. The Surrey Archaeological Society's first schedule of historic buildings was compiled in 1913 (Plate 37).

'Building and Gardening with Wit'

The growing appreciation of the vernacular architecture of Surrey, and of both its cultivated and 'wild' scenery, became an important influence on domestic architecture and designed landscapes. As early as 1803 the professional architect Richard Elsam considered that in Kent and Surrey house designers 'required no other guide' than its heritage of simple, traditional building. Not until the 1860s, when the histrionic styles of the Gothic Revival were falling into disfavour, was the existing domestic building of South-East England eagerly studied once more, so revealing the proportion, balance and graceful simplicity of half-timbered and stone-built houses. The masterly

98

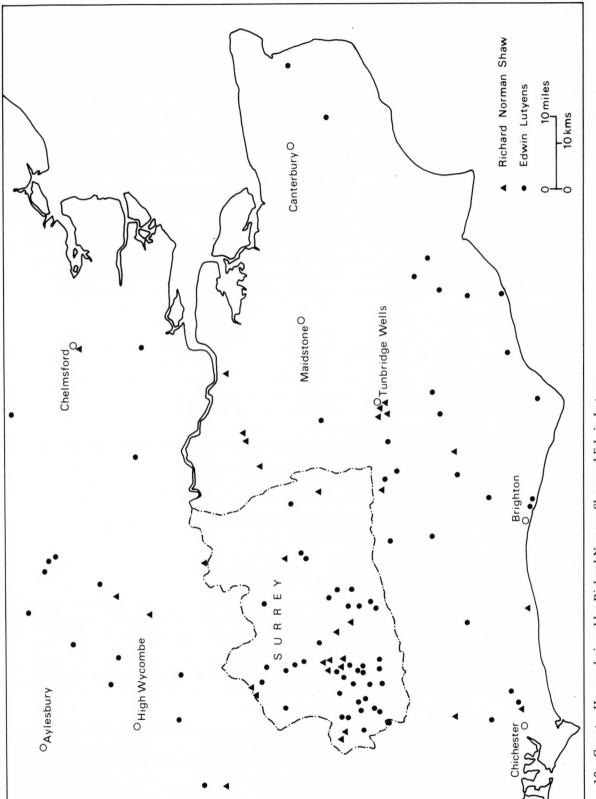

Map 10. Country Houses designed by Richard Norman Shaw and Edwin Lutyens.

Canterbury○

Chelmsford○

Maidstone○

Tunbridge Wells○

Brighton○

S U R R E Y

Aylesbury○

High Wycombe○

Chichester○

Richard Norman Shaw ▲

Edwin Lutyens ●

0   10 miles
0   10 kms

Pierrepoint, Farnham, by Richard Norman Shaw

attention given by traditional builders to details such as chamfers, stops, beams and joints was also noted, as the way in which the houses seemed to 'grow' organically from their settings.

Norman Shaw (1831–1912), who changed all our domestic architecture, and two of his pupils, Mervyn McCartney and Ernest Newton, were leaders of the movement towards the recreation of the style and building techniques of indigenous Wealden architecture, even to the extent of incorporating open halls, great hearths and chimneys, pargetting, braced beams, immense bay windows, deep cornices and bracketted barge boards. The chief inspiration of these architects for the new type of small country home was the Wealden house and particularly those nearest to London. Young architects wishing to make a national reputation drove a trap or cycled down deep woody Wealden byways searching at every lane's turning for vernacular survivals as models for their pattern books. Shaw, as a young man, worked in the office of G. E. Street, an architect who has left a deep mark on Surrey with his numerous churches and whose home, 'Holmdale' (1873), at Holmbury St. Mary is delightfully set on a wooded hillside. Shaw's own flair for recreating comfortable and sensibly planned country houses for the *nouveau riche* is illustrated by 'Pierrepoint', near Frensham (1870), 'Merrist Wood', Guildford (1877), and 'Hallams', Shamley Green (1894–5).

Edwin Lutyens (1869–1944) was the most brilliant of the second generation of Weald-inspired architects. His boyhood was spent at Thursley amidst many fine old Surrey houses on the verge of the west Surrey heaths. It was Lutyens' achievement to recreate the sense of prosperity, homeliness, ease and shapely beauty in the revival of the traditional style of country house. His earliest houses, such as 'Orchards', near Godalming, 'Goddards' on Abinger Common, and 'Tichbourne', beneath Hindhead, all built in the vast upsurge of Victorian building in Surrey, were all constructed of the local brick and stone of the country and were inspired by the visible Elizabethan and Jacobean masoncraft of their neighbourhoods.

Lutyens' first major commission was 'Munstead Wood', near Godalming, built for his cousin, Gertrude Jekyll (1843–1932) in 1896. In the work of this artist and gardener the influence of her west Surrey 'spirit of place' is even stronger than in Lutyens. She lived her long life at Bramley and Munstead amongst the exceptionally variegated landscape of heaths, woods, orchards and river meadows. It was a veritable 'wild garden' of a landscape thanks to its geological diversity and was aptly likened by her to a 'cosmic wonderland'. Always at the back of her mind was the image of a garden melting imperceptibly into woodland. 'Such a bit of wild forest in the small

100

valley and the hilly land beyond are precious lessons in the best way of tree and shrub planting.'

She was strongly influenced in her artistic consciousness by J. M. W. Turner, John Ruskin, and H. B. Brabazon, and also by the touch of 'careless freedom' of the Impressionists. She was also visibly inspired by the old-fashioned Surrey cottage gardens crowded with informally grouped hardy plants. Such gardens were becoming better known in England through the medium of Helen Allingham's and Birkett Foster's watercolours. Both these artists lived for a time at Witley: Foster is buried in the churchyard. To Gertrude Jekyll, naturally arranged groups of plants as in the wild and in cottage gardens were a form of gardening translated into terms of painting: 'planting gardens is like painting the landscape with living things'. The cottage gardens and her familiar Surrey wildscape are both closely mirrored in her garden designs and with an artist's eye she drew greatly upon them, in particular for her teaching of sympathetic colour planning and grouping.

Gertrude Jekyll

Another strong influence on Gertrude Jekyll was William Robinson (1838-1935), the author of *The Wild Garden* (1870) and innumerable works on landscape gardening and forestry, whose uncommon energy touched every aspect of arranging plants in bold, natural groupings. Jekyll helped Robinson to re-establish the herbaceous border in place of formally 'bedding out' tender summer plants such as geraniums and salvias. Her partnership with Edwin Lutyens, her many contributions to *The Garden* (edited by William Hudson), and her many books spread her garden prescriptions across the face of England. Many of her ideas are to be seen in such gardens open to the public as the Royal Horticultural Society's at Wisley, Vita Sackville-West's at Sissinghurst, Kent, 'Nymans', at Handcross, Sussex, and at 'Bodnant', Caernarvonshire (Plate 38).

Another contemporary landscape contribution to Surrey was the planting up of barren land with trees and the display of the vast reservoirs of hardy exotics brought back by collectors from the cool and temperate parts of the world. Surrey is particularly associated with this establishment of arboreta and pineta. G. F. Wilson began his famous Wisley Garden (now the Royal Horticultural Society's) in 1878. Like many of the new gardeners, he was a wealthy merchant, a candle manufacturer by trade, one of the many important businessmen in Surrey. He chose a wild and sandy spot and created a magnificent tree collection. His passion for arboreta spread like wildfire in west Surrey where the acid, sandy soils were highly suitable. The making of the Winkworth arboretum (now owned by the National Trust) by Dr. Wilfrid Fox after the Second World War marks the end

101

of an era. Landowners had become more and more fascinated by species of rhododendron and azalea and in scenes of almost unbelievable brilliance and splendour conveying an allusion of the Nilgiri Hills of Southern India or Sino-Himalaya rather than the west Surrey hills, one can still recapture something of the excitement by which Surrey plant collectors examined and discussed each new collection of seeds brought back from remote and previously unvisited parts of South-East Asia, China and Japan by such adventurous plant hunters as E. H. Wilson, George Forest and Frank Kingdon-Ward. Fittingly, such Surrey landscapes of the Age of Empire close some 300 years of landscape making. It is strange that man's last end in Surrey has been shaped in Nature's first beginnings (Plate 41).

The many open spaces still remaining within the present built-up area of Greater London are due to their rescue in the 18th and 19th centuries from appropriation for 'eligible villas', railway lines and buildings such as sewerage works and other public utilities. Although the Metropolitan Commons Act (1866) provided for the management of such urban commons as places for public recreation, so great a desire was generally expressed to select places of residence within easy reach of London that lords of manors were tempted to purchase tenants' rights of common with the intention of selling off land for building or other profitable purposes. The loss of commonland in Surrey by this process was very great. Railway companies eagerly sought commons because of their cheapness. The London and South Western and the London, Brighton and South Coast railway companies cut Wandsworth Common into ribbons, and Barnes, Mitcham and Tooting commons were disfigured. Other commons were lost, or threatened, by building proposals. The Commons Preservation Society, founded in 1866, stepped into the struggle to save those remaining. Fierce legal battles ensued which protracted up to 10 to 15 years, during which the Society and defendants contested costly actions, frequently argued before the Court of Appeal and even the appeal committee of the House of Lords. It is to the stubborn resistance of the Society, and commoners of like foresight, that the survival of Clapham, Wimbledon and other commons is due.

One of the most eventful chapters in the rescue of London commons was the successful fight for Banstead Downs, some 1,300 acres of heath and rough grazing on the summit of the North Downs, a prize second only to Epping Forest, secured earlier. In 1865 the lord of the manor responded to local feeling by agreeing to dedicate this magnificent open space to the public, but on his death his trustees sold the lord's common rights in Banstead manor to Sir John Hartropp, a Yorkshire baronet, who had taken residence in the vicinity and

Edward Lutyens

102

wished to sell off the commons for building. Hartropp's aim to extinguish rights of common by buying them up was thwarted by the impossibility of identifying all the claimants, many of whom occupied farms far away at Leigh and Horley 'in the Weald' or 'below the hill' in Chaldon. Such farmers no longer exercised their right to de-pasture sheep on the distant downland commons, but they nevertheless retained this privilege by virtue of the historic organisation of space in Surrey which, as we have seen, can be traced back to the dim beginnings of human life in the county. It is significant that this hard-fought legal action, begun in 1876, but not concluded until 1889, when the unanimous judgement of the Court of Appeal reversed an earlier judgement in favour of the defendant, was really won by the enduring influence of the distant past on the changing circumstances of the present.

The Call of High Places

From the 1870s there was a growing awakening to the value of the remaining 'wastes' for the purpose of outdoor recreation which had resisted the struggles of pioneer farmers with fire and plough. Tired City clerks perched on stools inhaling orange-coloured fogs and sooty air perceived Surrey increasingly as one vast open space for the enjoyment and recreation of Londoners. A. H. Sidgwick in his *Walking essays* (1912) has aptly summarised the strength of this important social movement in Surrey: 'Take a single bit of road, such as that in the Mole valley by Burford Bridge. To the walker it is a quiet interlude between the classical austerity of the Roman road [a disused stretch of the Stane Street running over the Mickleham Downs] and the more romantic interest of Denbies and Ranmore Common. To the motorist it is a brief moment in the morning scorch to Lewes . . . To the cyclist it is the last lap before the second shandy-gaff. To the Boxhill picnicker it is the way to heaven; to the Meredithian, the road to Mecca. One and all can meet on this ground and speak to each other in passing'.

As soon as the crank was applied to the bicycle the Sunday cycling clubs took to Surrey roads. The racers' preference was for speeding machines along the Brighton road. Clubmen took the 'Ripley road', as they called the 24-mile stretch of the Portsmouth Road from London. A. C. Pemberton in *The Complete Cyclist* (1897) noted that 'thousands of wheelmen and women pass through Kingston-on-Thames every Sunday', many proposing to lunch at *The Anchor* or other inns crowding the street at Ripley. Another favourite cycling tour was to Godstone, which involved all but expert cyclists in dismounting at

An early cyclist (after H. G. Wells', The Wheels of Chance)

103

Late nineteenth century sportsmen (after H. G. Wells', The Wheels of Chance*)*

Titsey Hill. These early cyclists were normally obliged to keep to the good surfaces of high roads. Pearson's *Athletic Record* (1896) supplied cycling maps which indicate that cyclists could not pursue their hobby through the most picturesque districts at that time because the surface of minor roads was too poor.

It was the rambler and hiker who first discovered, with the help of successively improved editions of the Ordnance Survey One Inch map, the joys of walking Surrey footpaths and byways. On account of its proximity to the West End and the variety of unspoilt scenery (and hence varied bodily exercise), Surrey offered the best of walking within reach of a day's excursion from London. Late Victorian men of letters were great walkers: Carlyle, R. L. Stevenson, Leslie Stephen, Hilaire Belloc and George Meredith, for example, were all devotees of Surrey rambling. The most famous walking society ever founded was that known as the Sunday Tramps. This regularly took a day's walk in Surrey. Meredith records one of these outings in 1880 accompanied by Leslie Stephen of the Bloomsbury Group. the founder; M. F. Pollock, the historian Croom Robertson, James C. Robertson, amongst others, 'and Hock, Appolinaris and cold sausages'. If Leslie Stephen is the 'patron saint' of ramblers, then his shrine is somewhere in that wonderful triangle of walking country bounded by Guildford, Leatherhead and Leith Hill. Another distinguished Surrey rambler was 'Walker Miles' (Edmund Seyfang-Taylor) who wrote innumerable walking guides at the beginning of this century, and whose memorial is appropriately at the top of Leith Hill tower. Yet of all the Surrey walkers none deserves more recognition than Meredith. On his long customary walks, or pacing like a shipman in the sight of the matchless panorama at 'Flint Cottage' he caught the quintessence of Surrey scenery and transfused it into his poems and novels. He joined the happy, rain-beaten ramblers who ate their sandwiches on Leith Hill, or the jovial and sweaty bands who flocked to Gomshall cafés for huge watercress teas, and some of Meredith's own characters who were also great walkers, such as Richard Feverell and Arthur Rhodes, were probably living incarnations of some of these acquaintances. 'It is self-evident that nothing educates the eye for the feature of a landscape so well as the practice of measuring it by your own legs', wrote Stephen. It follows from this that the Surrey landscape will not again be appreciated so perceptively as it was at the end of the last century until its present guardians file through it as rucksacked ramblers instead of unobservantly speeding past it in a motor car.

104

XVII *The Old Rural Society (1840-1918)*

With Gertrude Jekyll's delightful *Old west Surrey* (1904) we can in imagination recall the contemporary Surrey country people and their cottages. Cottages and little farms still survived with the traditional bacon loft built into the great living room chimney (where the flitches were stored until they were deliciously smoked). About the broad firesides (adapted to wood-burning) were handsome chimney cranes on which pots were suspended over the fire, cast-iron fire-dogs and chimney backs. Older folk still treasured their heavy oak furniture— tables, forms, dressers, and large oaken 'linen-hutches' on the bare floors of the upstairs rooms, and four-poster beds with spotless hangings and lavender-scented sheets. In stone-floored kitchens and cider cellars, well-scoured wooden trenchers, old stoneware and leather harvest bottles lined the shelves of white elm dressers. A rose-trained porch led into the flower-borders giving off the scent of lupins, stocks, wallflowers, heartsease, and several sweet-smelling shrubs and herbs. In the kitchen garden, shading pig-sty and henroost, were sturdy fruit-trees of the old-fashioned variety such as ribstone and golden-pippin, Blenheim orange, codling, russet, as well as cherry, and possibly also medlar and quince. These cottagers went out and worked hard to earn a living. They kept a large family, yet provided for their old age by saving a little, and at their death were still able to leave something for their children.

Timber and brick granary on 'steddles'

Numerous examples still survive of the old Surrey farmhouses and cottages with their traditional barns. The typical Surrey cottage in the 18th century outside the 'stone' district of west Surrey was weather-boarded on the ground floor and provided with a tile-hung upper storey and tile roof. The weather-boarding was not original, but added when beams shrank and let in draughts and rain. Some were entirely built of timber, painted white in local fashion, for example 'Red Lodge' and Manor Farm at Claygate. Barns were built of timber, tarred for weather protection, and were often of large size, seven or eight bays in length, with oak piers and pantile roofs.

In stone districts more substantial buildings exist. The 'tithe' barns in Witley and Shalford have been converted into houses with the minimum of alteration. The former is a huge building of six bays with an aisle running the full length of the west side. At Shalford a group of former agricultural buildings—'tithe' barn, cow byre, cowman's

Timber granary on 'steddles'

The barn, Oxenford Grange, Elstead by A. W. Pugin, c. 1840

and shepherd's cottages—have also recently been adapted to modern residences in an imaginative and sympathetic manner. The great stone barn at Oxenford Grange, Elstead, on an estate owned by the Cistercians of Waverley before the Dissolution, was designed by the famous revivalist architect, Augustus Pugin, *c.* 1840, in the 13th-century style of the great barns still surviving at Beaulieu in the New Forest and at Great Coxton near Lechlade, Gloucestershire. It is the finest re-creation of the medieval scene in Surrey, a beautiful, and even moving, vision of the past (Plate 35).

Water-mills were often large wooden structures of great beauty such as Newark Mill, near Ripley (recently destroyed by fire), or Castle Mill, Dorking. Haybarns were constructed on rat-proof stone piers ('steddles'), and half-timbered, 'brick-nogged' granaries were also similarly constructed. In the Weald a stone causeway would run from the road up to the door of the farmhouse, because in wet weather the path was almost impassable. Wealden farms and cottages were normally roofed in the flaggy varieties of Horsham Stone. These heavy slabs, delightfully mellowed by weathering and moss, are so durable that many existing buildings still retain their original roofing, as is indicated by a liberal amount of soot on its underside, derived from the hall fire of the farmstead before the 'lofting-over' of the hall during the 'Great Rebuilding' of the 16th and 17th centuries. Many of the more substantial half-timbered and stone roofed farmhouses, picturesque with their fine gables, oriel windows, porches, and vestiges of moats, were bought at the end of the 19th century by London merchants and professional people who converted them into 'gentlemen's residences'. Thus by the Edwardian period it was very rare for one of the accessible oak and stone-roofed farmhouses of Surrey to be still occupied by a farmer who farmed the attached land.

One of the anciently-established rhythms of Surrey country life was the seasonal migration of the poor as hired harvest hands to the Sussex cornlands or to the Farnham and Kent hop fields. This custom was facilitated by the unusual prolongation of the harvest in South-East England because of the variegated soil types and consequently wide range of crops, each with their differing ripening periods. Consequently a casual labourer could follow the regional harvests. The hay harvest of outer London was the earliest. Then followed the corn harvest of the Isle of Wight and the Sussex Coastal Plain, which was followed by that of fruit and hops. In winter there was coppice work. As in the Sussex Weald, this migratory custom was probably well established by the late 14th century. For generations the practice resolved the real difficulty for the large landed estate of the seasonal mobility of labour. By the 18th and 19th centuries it is well documented, none

106

better than in Sturt's writings. In his day the hired helpers walked in bands all night in readiness for the start of work soon after sunrise. For several weeks the hired bands would sleep in barns or out in the open, and then made a jolly journey back with their hard-earned fortune. Few other events in the labourer's year would have provided so much adventure. With their money the harvest hands would buy boots or clothes for the winter, or a cartload of wood for turning. Sturt's rather romantic picture of the late-19th-century seasonal harvester is doubtless authentic, but between 1780 and 1850 when many Surrey parishes had more than their fair share of worldly misery we must probably visualise the Surrey labourer desperately combing the countryside for harvest work, so marked was the geographical unevenness of economic progress and population distribution in the South-East at that time.

Surrey bread oven and salt hole (after Surrey Vernacular Architecture Group)

The traditional sources of harvest labour in Surrey were the areas of large cottage-bounded commons. The heath parishes around Farnham were half-emptied of able-bodied men in summer. The cottagers, many of them 'squatters' with no legal title to land, cut fern to provide litter for their pigs and cattle, and grew a little wheat in their gardens which was ground at the local mill and baked in bread-ovens heated with furze. These people were called 'broom squires'. S. Baring-Gould's *The Broom-Squires* (1896), a topographical novel with a setting near Hindhead in the late 18th century, is a reminder of the time when it was a wild region with scattered dwellings along the streams with little hedged gardens and bright green meadows forming small islands amidst the sea of fern and heather. These small 'waste edge' colonies still retain much of their outward aspect though little of the former social atmosphere is retained. 'Broom squires' were not wedded to the place they inhabited, as Sturt noted, and only stayed if the heath gave them a chance of getting food and shelter. In bad winters such as those of 1878–9 and 1889–90 these people suffered great hardship when their chief crops failed, even to extent of living on the verge of starvation.

The small tenant farmers of the Surrey Weald were also in great difficulties at this time on account of the import of cheap corn from overseas. Since the 1780s their fate has been chequered. The 'boom' war economy based on high corn prices collapsed in 1820 with a return to normal peace-time trading. The Surrey labourers' standard of living had improved during that time. Cottages were better furnished than formerly and cottagers lived better, notably consuming more bacon, wheaten bread, tea, coffee and sugar. Between 1820 and the 1840s the labourers and small farmers were severely depressed. Farmers paid off labourers and Wealden parishes became eaten up with poor.

Poor rates rose to unprecedented levels, in some cases as much as four times the annual rent of the land. In the 1830s it was difficult to find tenants for Wealden farms and some landlords were obliged to advance money to tenants to enable them to take land. The soil required so much labour to put into readiness for a crop that in some years the expense of cultivation exceeded the return. In these conditions much land was taken out of cultivation and allowed to tumble to grass. In the late 19th century the general fall in corn prices was exacerbated in the Weald by successive wet seasons in the 1870s which caused outbreaks of foot-rot in sheep and prevented the customary fallowing indispensable for cereals.

Some of the most sensitive and observant pictures of Surrey country life ever penned were written by Denham Jordan under the pseudonym of 'Son of the marshes'. The little that is known of his career has to be extracted from the tantalisingly brief autobiographical details he permits himself in books on natural history of the Weald published between 1889 and 1898. His childhood was spent on the marshes of the Swale in north Kent. He travelled to the United States, but he had a deep familiarity with Surrey and Wealden Sussex. When he was recording his memoirs (edited, and possibly written, by Mrs. Owen Visgar, 'J. A. Owen') he was earning a living as a painter and decorator in Dorking, where he died in 1920. He wrote in the tradition of Richard Jefferies, W. H. Hudson and Edward Thomas, and although much less well known than these writers he can match, and indeed excel, them in the shrewdness of his observations and the charm of his style. In the absence of well-authenticated records of life of his time his books are a mine of information for the historian.

Jordan's great love was the wild country of fir and heather around Dorking, the great heaths on the Hampshire border, or the forested country of the deep Weald. In his walks into the latter he delineates with great clarity the woodlanders and their simple ways of life. They rose before sunrise, and the cycle of tree-felling, copse-cutting, hoop-shaving, hurdle-making, charcoal burning, and bark-stripping kept them employed all year, in contrast to farmhands in corn districts who were generally laid off for part of the winter. They often travelled eight miles a day to and from their place of work and when work necessitated a longer stay they camped out in 'forest' style by making a shanty thatched with fern and provided with a wattle door packed with heather.

Timber-frame of charcoal burner's sleeping hut. (after J. R. Armstrong, Open Air Museum, Singleton)

As late as the 1880s the remoter parts of Surrey retained, as far at least as outward appearances went, their aspect and ways of life of centuries ago. People often still paid for services in kind: the village shoemaker would take payment in farm produce, for example. Stocks

108

still stood on village greens; each farm still possessed a limekiln. Communities yet retained some individual characteristics and dialects peculiar to themselves and were moulded by their different environments as much as they moulded them. Thus the Surrey Wealdsman was slow of speech (though his wits were keen). His movements were also rather slow and ponderous, but his long stride and perfect balance enabled him to cover wet, slippery clays with agility. Generally, Weald folk were sturdy, well-built people because puny persons could not have done their work. The men of the heaths (the fir and heather districts) such as the fern-cutters and stone-diggers, tended to keep themselves apart from the woodlanders, as did also those of the wortlebury (hurt) woods near Peaslake. These latter were particularly uncommunicative people addicted to smuggling and other illegal activities and were taught from childhood 'to see everything but to say nothing'. Distinguishable again were the country people north of the Downs.

Farm wagon of the type built at George Sturt's wheelwright's shop, Farnham

Other masterpieces of recording 19th-century social change in Surrey are the works of George Sturt ('George Bourne') of Farnham, who took over the management of his father's wheelwright's business in 1884. His *Bettesworth Book* (1901) and *Memoirs of a Surrey Labourer* (1907) were followed by *Change in the Village* (1912) and *The Wheelwright's Shop* (1923). It is through Sturt's perceptive understanding of the rapidly-changing rural civilisation of his times (so superior to much of that which passes today as 'rural sociology') that we know something of the nature of traditional Surrey craftsmanship. By his day, generations of Surrey people had created a tradition of handicrafts using local raw materials such as wood-turning, pottery and glass-making. As a master wheelwright at Farnham, Sturt felt he knew enough of the nature of craftsmanship to distrust the ideas of William Morris and Walter Crane who 'set too much upon Art products and two little upon the Artist'. The 'rotarius' returned in an occasional Surrey Poll Tax Return of 1379 is usually the first recorded reference to the wheelwright trade. The craft of wheel-maker, like that of charcoal burner, was often handed down from father to son for generations. Sturt's chronicle of the working lives of individual craftsmen is moving and enlightening and it is skilfully interwoven to show their share in the advancement of what was then the little town of Farnham, and their intimacy with the peculiar needs of the neighbourhood which was their local market. 'In farm wagon or dung-cart, barley-roller, plough, water-barrel, or what not, the dimensions we chose, the curves we followed . . . were imposed upon us by the nature of the soil in this or that farm, the temper of this or that customer, or his choice perhaps in horseflesh.'

XVIII The Surrey Side of London
(1840-1918)

Bermondsey Abbey, remnant of the tower

By the early 18th century Surrey nearest to London had become a great purveyor to the metropolis. 'Dorking' fowls from the Wealden smallholders; delicious, sweet 'Banstead' mutton, fattened on all the farms within a 20-mile radius of the City; vegetables from the market-gardens of Battersea and Lambeth; fresh milk from hundreds of cow-keepers in Camberwell, Peckham, Brixton and beyond; and immense quantities of pigs fed on the waste from the riverside starch factories and corn distilleries; all this food poured into the London wholesale markets. It was not until late Georgian times that the insatiable demand for building sites within the capital began to drive out the Surrey market-gardeners and cowkeepers. The first stage of this invasion is marked by the building of Westminster Bridge in 1750 and its new approach roads leading to Dover, Brighton and Portsmouth, such as the 'Wash way' across Lambeth Marsh which led to the Brixton Causeway, also on low-lying ground. These were the great coaching arteries along which houses first slowly crept in the 1780s and then were to envelop completely the ancient tightly-clustered and well-filled villages of Camberwell, Peckham, Stockwell, Streatham and Clapham. Rocque's map of 1762 is a fine rendering of this phase. For the next two generations, the advance of building was gradual and piecemeal. Coach travellers in the 1790s still glimpsed fine villas such as 'Grove Hill', Camberwell, or 'Loughborough House', in Brixton, amidst market gardens backed by the gently-rising wooded hills of Norwood. 'Grove Hill' was for 40 years one of the most famous sights on the Brighton road.

A second stage in the suburbanisation of the old villages in north-east Surrey was the enclosure of the common lands of the manor of Lambeth in 1806. This met with fierce resistance. The commons were of great recreational value to the citizens of London and Westminster across the Thames. It was also argued that drovers supplying the London markets would be deprived of essential resting-places for their livestock. In short, the commons of this corner of Surrey had long been an essential part of London life. Nevertheless, the Enclosure Award allotted Norwood and Kennington Commons into plots suitable for building. As late as this time, as Horwood's fine map of 1799 demonstrates, Kennington marked the end of built-up London, and even in 1824 the Oval was the furthest limit of houses. By the 1830s

110

a full-scale invasion was in progress. New streets laid out in Stockwell, Brixton and Norwood became outposts of London between four to six miles from the Thames, and Tulse Hill, Camberwell, Peckham, Dulwich, Clapham and Streatham were spreading amoeba-like towards each other. By 1868 they were solidly part of London. The market gardeners were driven further afield towards Morden and Walton-on-Thames or to Hampton in Middlesex, under the advance of the steady tide of building, as is shown by Cassell's map of South London. Camberwell quadrupled its population between 1801 and 1831; Clapham, fast-growing with the building of Vauxhall Bridge, tripled in size during the same period. These examples show the scale of the ever-increasing tide of urban development. Still building went on furiously. By 1900 the built-up edge of London stood 10 to 12 miles from the Thames, and Esher Green was almost the first strip of 'countryside' glimpsed by travellers on the Southampton railway. The 'Surrey side of London' had become by then a great suburban continent, the largest urban concentration which the world had ever seen.

Lambeth water-front (1886)

Many must have witnessed with anguish the blotting out of the lovely south bank countryside. One who has written sadly of this experience is John Ruskin (1819–1900), one of the most widely read and admired of all Victorian writers on the art of the human environment. His father's practice was to take summer lodgings for his family in Dulwich or Hampstead as a change from the air of Brunswick Square, a convention which dates from the early 18th century, as we have seen. In 1823 he bought a new villa on the top of Herne Hill, one of only two pairs of houses existing there. This again was typical of development in South London at this time. 'The main army', said a contemporary, 'is preceded by an advance of villas . . . seizing a few picked positions. Then come the more solid ranks of the semi-detached . . . along the high roads and in the neighbourhood of railway stations.' As Ruskin grew older he witnessed the streams and meadow ditches of his youth putridly bricked-over, the ponds drained, the hedgerows and copses grubbed up and burned, the farmhouses demolished. As the local railway stations were opened the new railways brought hordes of 'expiating roughs' by every excursion train to view the Crystal Palace. The 'politely inhabited groves' of which he writes in his autobiography *Præterita* were the haunts of well-do-do London tradesmen, usually possessing 'a great cortège of footmen and glitter of plate, extensive pleasure grounds, costly hot-houses and carriages driven by coachmen in wigs', and whose ladies dashed up to doors in a barouche. Down the hill were the small shopkeepers of the Walworth Road, and behind them were the houses of the poor towards

An example of Lambeth stoneware by Louisa E. Edwards of Doulton's, 1877

the Thames, unseen by the counting-house clerks who daily took the horse-drawn omnibus into the self-satisfied City of the late 19th century (Plates 42 and 43).

In Brixton the pavements crept further and further from London. Loughborough House ended its days as a finishing school for the 'sons of gentlemen' before being demolished in 1853 to make way for more than 70 houses built in 1854–5. In Loughborough Road the ground landlord specified houses 'not inferior to third rate'; 'fourth rate' houses as defined by the current Metropolitan Building Act being built in side streets. Few of the present inhabitants of Brixton today have the means of living in Victorian third- and fourth-raters. A 'third-rate house' was a rather splendidly dignified semi-detached residence with a minimum of six large rooms; these are now being modernised and let as two or even more tenements. The 'fourth-rate' houses are tending to be replaced by modern flats. A little earlier than the Loughborough district 'an immense quantity of new building' sprang up in north Brixton at Angell Town where its new district church was begun in 1845 (Plate 47).

By the 1880s the poverty and squalor of the Surrey waterside was notorious. Richard Jefferies' *Red roofs of London* affords a glimpse of the catacombs of Bermondsey viewed by the daily stream of travellers in trains rattling along the arched embankments passing level with garrets containing 'women and children with scarce room to move, the bed and dining-table in the same apartment'. In the backward glance of time, Gustave Doré and Cruikshank have by their sardonic sketches left an imperishable memory of the South London poor in such vivid scenes. It is, however, from Charles Booth's *Life and labour of the people of London* that we obtain the most accurate and vivid descriptions of social life in the streets converging towards the Elephant and Castle, the hub of the new South London. His elaborately annotated maps show the wide highroads coloured bright red to signify well-to-do middle-class inhabitants or small shopkeepers, and in imagination we can visualise these roads crammed with the new clanging trams jostling with horse-drawn omnibuses and cabs. The poorer streets ran off these carriage roads and as the oldest inhabited areas nearest the river bank were reached they degenerated into dark, noisome alleys and nests of courts. The most notorious of these ghettoes was Jacob's Island in Bermondsey, Dickens's grim setting for the pursuit and death of Bill Sykes in *Oliver Twist*, but the vice, poverty and overcrowding in St. Saviour's, Southwark, almost matched it. Another example, typical of these crowded, foul, alleys was Black Alley, comprising 14 tiny tenements behind the *Black Bear* inn in Kentish Street, Newington. When people 'got a bit decent' they rented

41. This delightful garden at Holmbury-St.-Mary is indicative of many country houses established there in the Victorian Age.

42. View of the site of the Crystal Palace from Penge Wood, early 19th century.

43.   Norwood, before the eruption of housing in the mid 19th century.

44.   P. Gustave Doré's sardonic bird's eye view from the steam railways threading through South London of the interminable terraces, potteries and work-yards which were the haunts of the poor (1872).

45.   Rotherhithe in the mid-19th century.

46.   Hayfields, a dairy or two and a market-garden gave people near London the illusion that they were in the countryside.

47. The telefoto lens captures the whole of the 'Surrey side of London' from Brixton. The Big Ben tower of the House of Commons is on the extreme right and the Highgate and Hampstead Hills form the background.

48. Aerial view of the historic core of Guildford. High and North Streets extend diagonally behind the Castle Keep. Large and wrongly sited modern buildings (a multi-storey car park--top; department stores—bottom and centre) and shopping centres threaten to disintegrate the old quarters completely.

a house in Clapham or Sydenham; the less successful remained. Although the great riverside belt of the south bank was uniformly characterised by the poverty and squalor grimly manifest in the streets, its local life was based on a number of distinct communities which kept blazingly alive the strong loyalties of a village. The Borough High Street and its vicinity, including Tabard Street, was famous for its inns—over 200 of them—the relic of the coaching days when travellers entering and leaving London by the Old Kent Road took lodgings there. Here, too, lived the Billingsgate porters, extraordinary bundles of human energy, who ran to and from the ships and railway vans, and many hundreds of costermongers who supplied in street markets most of the wants of the poor. Further east, Bermondsey was the home of leather-workers and tanners. Rotherhithe had its ship-chandlers about the docks, its fish-curers and basket-makers and a great colony of Irish stevedores, orderly and hard-working by day, but rolling drunk in the streets by night, brawling and going about in hooligan gangs. Between Blackfriars Bridge and Lambeth Palace, in the shadow of the great railway stations, lived an army of cabmen and 'costers', not all as picturesque as the pearly-buttoned and be-plumed costers of story and song, for some were so poor that they carried their own wares, being unable to afford either donkey or barrow. South again one encountered the Lambeth potteries and food factories where in a single street the air was charged with the delicious vapours of strawberry jam mixed with the stench of boiling fat, tannin and vinegar. Here the highway of the Thames, crowded with the merchandise of the whole world shipped up its river, and plied by innumerable 'penny' steamers, was lined by the shabbiest, blackest and ugliest buildings imaginable, chiefly decayed and ruinous warehouses that had lost their trade to the docks downstream (Plates 39, 44, 45).

Meanwhile, the outer suburbs of London were developing. The effects of railway construction on the location of new housing estates in the vicinity of Kingston-upon-Thames is particularly interesting. The old borough of Kingston opposed the building of the Nine Elms and Woking railway (later extended to Southampton) in the interest of its coaching trade. The railway line was built instead in ·1838 through Surbiton, in a remote corner of Kingston parish, and then almost entirely rural. The first station was named 'Kingston', though it was three miles away from the town. From a small estate by the station Surbiton rapidly grew to a population of 15,000 by 1901 and in the manner of a 'high-class' suburb was plentifully endowed with large Gothic churches and good shops. Shortly afterwards New Malden (to distinguish it from the old agricultural settlement nearby) mushroomed around Christ Church, built in 1866. This town was

Late Victorian tourists, (after H. G. Wells', The Wheels of Chance)

113

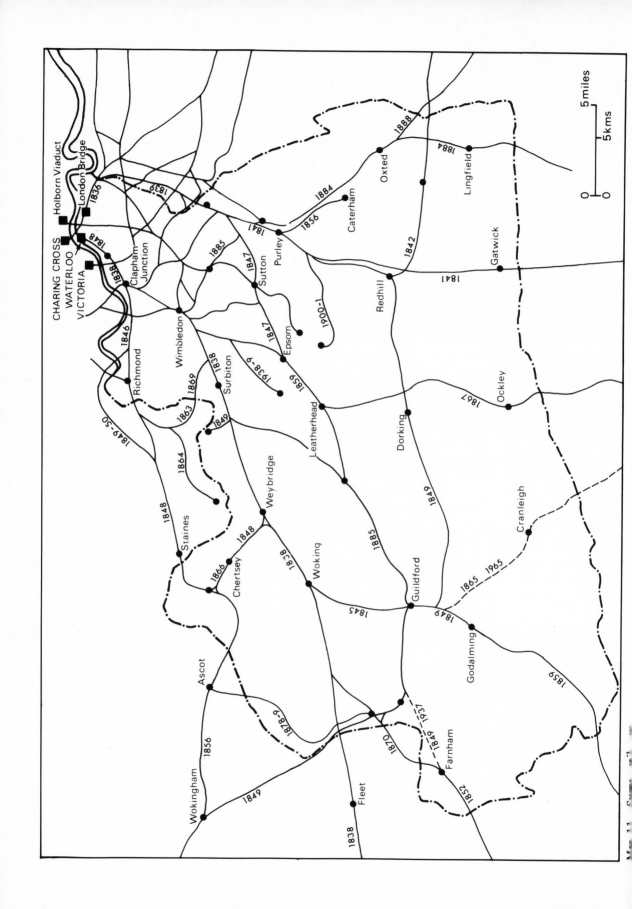

Map 11   Surrey railways

never served by express trains, and consequently residential property tended to be of a cheaper variety. Kingston Hill came on to the building market in the 1850s and new villas sprang up when Norbiton station was opened in 1863. In 1878 this 'smart' estate erected its own church (St. Paul's), a common practice of the time, although the parish church of St. Peter's, Norbiton, was very close (Map 11, p. 114).

A cyclist

A further stage in urbanisation was reached when villages further from London were 'developed' when the 'New Line' from London to Guildford via Leatherhead was opened in 1885. Claygate and Oxshott (on attractive heathland) then spread around their respective stations. By the 1880s many of the middle-class Londoners either could not afford, or felt submerged rather than freed in the new but somewhat anonymous inner south-west and north London, and they therefore acquired a partiality for suburban life. This process, with the help of the railways, evolved the more exclusive outer suburb with its villa residences, fast-growing lengths of laurel and laurustinus extending over the countryside. This soon attracted considerable literary attention. H. G.Wells's *Ann Veronica* (1909) cuttingly refers to a stuffiness and air of conscious elegance of Worcester Park.

In locomotion, the Surrey railways were fast superseding road traffic in mid Victorian times. Steam was first used for crossing the Weald in 1841, when the London to Brighton railway opened. Redhill sprang up around a railway station on this line and with the construction of branch lines to Reading and Ashford speculative land companies so successfully 'boomed' its railway advantages that the modern town of Redhill had by 1861 outstripped in population its mother town of Reigate, a typical decaying coaching town. In few Surrey places is the juxtaposition of the Victorian and ealier ages, and the differing social, political, architectural and economic values they embodied, so vividly contrasted as in this once single parish. It was also a symptom of the too rapidly urbanising environment which has since dislocated Surrey.

The origin of Woking is the strangest of the Surrey towns created in the Age of Steam. In 1838 a railway station of the London and Southampton railway was opened on heathland. The Necropolis Company purchased about one quarter of Woking parish as the first and largest necropolis under the London Necropolis Act of 1852 which provided for the burial of London citizens beyond the confines of the metropolis for reasons of health. Thus Surrey was providing space not only for London's living but also for its dead, conveyed 25 miles by steam train to their final resting place. The government also assigned to Woking public buildings being erected under the various reforming acts such as convict prisons and a lunatic asylum.

115

XIX The Austere Present

. . . London, that great sea, whose ebb and flow
At once is deaf and loud, and on the shore
Vomits its wrecks, and still howls for more.
Yet in its depths what treasures!

> Shelley,
> *Letter to Maria Gisborne* (1820)

Recessed window of a suburban house, late nineteenth century

Change in Surrey since the First World War has proceeded at an immense pace, and much of the county's face has changed out of all recognition. This has put the absorptive and adaptive tradition of the county to its severest test. Surrey has shared the many problems general to England which have been brought about by changes in the pattern of land ownership, the incidence of taxation, farming practice, economic and class structure and the demand from an increasingly urbanised community for greater space for industrial development and recreation. The location of Surrey in the most prosperous part of Britain, across the path of London's expansion to the south-west, has greatly exacerbated the difficulties. Inextricably Surrey has become drawn into the huge urban region that is London. The county's increase in population during the decade 1951–61 was the highest recorded— over 150,000—and the number of persons commuting to London almost doubled over the period 1951–71, from 77,000 to 150,000, representing 30 per cent. of the total employed. Surrey was placed in the mortal danger of being swallowed up like Middlesex, such was the drawing-power of London's commercial houses and the energy with which the London County Council and its successor the Greater London Council dispersed the population of inner London. Surrey adapted itself unevenly, and often reluctantly, but, on the whole, successfully, to these changes. That Surrey has survived its greatest crisis is largely due to the concept of the Metropolitan Green Belt, the primary barrier erected against the tumbling disorder of a metropolis on the move. This idea developed out of the voluntary preservation of Surrey's countryside before the Second World War. The Belt has had a profound influence on the present character of Surrey, but the question for the future is whether the concept can still be maintained when powerful political and social forces are generating the biggest upheaval in thought and ways of life in England's history. The fate of Surrey is thus still in the balance.

116

During the years between the two World Wars motor cars and electric trains brought a further exodus out of London into rural Surrey. Many of the newcomers sought small houses and cottages as weekend homes. Their 'discovery' of clusters of plainly furnished cottages, still beautiful in their suggestion of traditional Surrey life, tended to fall into successive stages of development. The first London owners were often obliged to leave their cars at nearby farm stables for the weekend because remoter cottages were still served by unmade bridle or footpaths. It was to them an adventure to bring in provisions by wheelbarrow; to draw water from the well; to light the oil lamps; to heap aromatic wood on open hearths; and to share a lawn-mower with friends from Kensington across the meadow. Soon, however, came 'improvements'. The road was made up (perhaps even provided with a gutter) and garages and servants' wings were built on to cottages; new electricity generators made the oil lamps obsolete and a hard tennis court was laid out on an adjacent field. London tradesmen began calling at the door, bringing fresh produce from Billingsgate, Covent Garden and Smithfield, for although the Surrey countryside was itself well provisioned the Londoners tended to cut themselves off from the surrounding countryside and to live apart. The Piccadilly firm of Fortnum and Mason's made special deliveries of after-dinner coffee, and by 1928 the green delivery vans of Harrods of Kensington,

*Sheraton wardrobe,
Guildford*

'That go to every dwelling
By farm and fields and woods'

as the firm announced in its newspaper advertisements, became familiar all over Surrey on their journeys to 'London's border'.

This permeation of the Surrey countryside by migrants wedded to urban values brought further problems. By the late 1920s the centres of Surrey towns were congested by motor traffic to a dangerous degree. The West Surrey Regional Town Planning Advisory Committee recommended the building of by-passes and the construction of the Guildford and Godalming by-pass was completed in 1934 under a government scheme of public works to relieve unemployment in the county. Meanwhile, the destroying ugliness of the jerry builder was creeping like a cancer along the main roads. A sustained fight ensued to conserve some of the finest stretches of scenery in the county, and an incalculable debt is owed to the generosity of individuals who presented their estates to the National Trust, or who supported appeals for the purchase of land for the nation. The building up in successive stages of the National Trust estate of Box Hill is a striking example of what was achieved by purely voluntary effort. The first gift, and the jewel of the whole estate, was the summit of the hill, given by Mr. Leopold

117

Jacobean exterior chimney stack

Salomons of Norbury Park in 1914 as a memorial to George Meredith, who for more than 40 years resided below the Hill at 'Flint Cottage' and did his best work there. In 1921 Miss A. M. Warburg donated 'Lodge Hill' and 'Juniper Bottom' (Meredith's 'Happy Valley') and in 1923 a public appeal sponsored by *Country Life* led to the purchase of Ashurst Rough. The acquisition of the glorious White Hill in the Headley Valley was due to local initiative in 1926, and small gifts of highly valuable 'protecting' land followed. In 1935, as the result of a further national appeal launched by *Country Life* the land around Burford Lodge was purchased, so guarding the famous Whites. In 1939 Lord Beaverbrook presented land on Mickleham Downs adjoining White Hill. Since the War the Juniper Hall estate, 'Flint Cottage' and land on the southern slopes of Box Hill have been purchased for the Trust, the latest acquisition to date being in 1976 under the will of Mr. H. A. Gordon Clark. The Box Hill estate now forms a continuous unit comprising more than 900 acres actually owned by the Trust and another 300 acres under its protection. Other fragments of the fast-vanishing countryside preserved from 'improvement' were the Milford and Witley commons, the gift to the National Trust in 1921 by Mr. Thackeray Taylor, who succeeded his friend William Morris as secretary of the Society for the Protection of Ancient Buildings. The first step in efforts to preserve Leith Hill, also threatened by speculative building, was taken in 1929 when land was purchased from the proceeds of a public appeal sponsored by *The Times*. In 1930–31 local residents, including the composer Vaughan Williams, again prevented the erection of houses on the hill. It was by similar efforts that much of Hindhead was preserved. Thus it is that in Green-Belt Surrey the National Trust has so much to show. Local authorities also took the initiative of purchasing farmland to prevent it falling into the hands of builders. One of the most prudent purchases, and certainly the best known, is the fine stretch of the Mount on the left bank of the river Wey which overlooks the High Street in central Guildford, a symbolic gresture by the town which is so famous, and in part still beautiful, and proud of its country setting in the Wey Gap (Plate 4).

Since the Second World War there has been growing concern with the problems of country planning, the preservation of scenery, and the relation of buildings to their setting. The presence just across the county border of Heathrow and Gatwick, the two London airports, created severe congestion, much new building and a generally deteriorating environment. Nodal points on traffic arteries have become important centres for warehousing, such as Horley, Staines and Sunbury. Meanwhile the traffic of the London Docks greatly declined and the Surrey Docks, opened in 1700, have been completely closed. Surrey's historic rôle as a passageway between east and west is emphasised by the construction of motorways 3 and 4, and the partially-built motorways 23 and 25, all focussed on central London. These have been particularly difficult to fit into the gentle, flowing Surrey landscape on account of their width and vast intersections. The demands on Surrey for recreation have grown enormously with rising standards of living and the mobility conferred by the motor car. It is estimated that at least one quarter of the eight million residents of Greater London look to Surrey as their primary centre of recreation or pass through it annually on the way to the coast. In consequence several of the Surrey 'honey-pots' are over-used under the weekend impact of car-borne thousands, especially Box Hill, Leith Hill and Frensham Common, and almost everywhere the reconciliation of the conflicting demands of agriculture and recreation is a major problem. The designation of the North Downs and the Surrey Hills as Areas of Outstanding Beauty, together with a similar proposal for the High Weald and the designation of smaller areas of great landscape value, has given some measure of protection to these hard-pressed areas.

Majestic cedars and sham Grecian ruins, Virginia Water

The countryside itself is fast changing and safeguards against its destruction are made difficult when the county's urbanised community has a misplaced vision of farmers as unlucky persons who have not been able to escape hard work. Further problems arise from the particular character of the Surrey man-made landscape as it had evolved by 1918. Much of it fell within Karel Capek's description' 'the English countryside is not for work, it is for show. It is as green as a park and as immaculate as paradise'. The passing of the Villa civilisation and its dying race of landowners has meant that land is now again being commercially farmed under quite different management principles. Inevitably this has involved the wholesale removal of hedges and the destruction of many groups of trees. Many farms on poorer ground, especially in the Weald, which has always grudged a living to the small farmer on heavy clay, are no longer being farmed and are used as pony studs. Most of the attractive farmsteads not sold off earlier have been detached from landed estates and are used as residences by people who work in towns.

The aspect of the North Downs is changing with the cessation of sheep grazing and the recent decline of the rabbit population. Scrub has invaded and made public access more difficult, if not impossible. Many fine clumps of fir trees and stands of beech are over mature and slowly dying. Former open heather and fern-clad hills are now giving way to freely seeding Scots pine. Hedgerows and waysides once planted

119

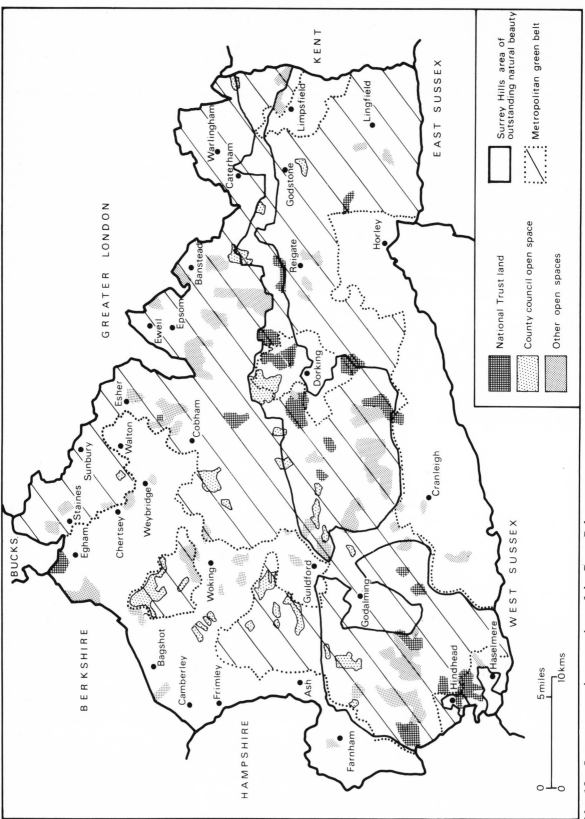

Map 12. Surrey: successive extensions of the Green Belt concept.

with fine elm and oak are no longer being adequately cared for. The spectre is that Surrey could change from a land of beauty to merely a land of beauty spots.

Since the War a wide range of light industry has developed. Scientific instruments, electrical engineering, printing and publishing, aircraft and motor car manufacture, food and drink, chemicals, and research laboratories are the most characteristic. Many of the firms have been displaced from inner and suburban areas of London by the rising cost of accommodation and labour. These same problems have induced commercial firms, with the government's active encouragement, also to move their headquarters from London to Guildford, Dorking, or Reigate. This industrial development and the residential growth since the inter-war years has spreadeagled the old Surrey towns into a sprawling mass. Their ubiquitous original form, as Rocque's map of Surrey demonstrates, was merely a short ribbon consisting of an old village street developed into the built-up section of a post road, the culminating point of which was the coaching inn (Plate 34).

Barn, Manor Lodge Farm, Claygate (1925)

Nevertheless, the worse excesses of change have been avoided by successive extensions of the Metropolitan Green Belt. This was conceived by Patrick Abercrombie in his Greater London Plan (1944). In 1972 two-thirds of Surrey then unbuilt over was covered by the Green Belt acting as a barrier to London's outward growth, and by a further extension in 1974 nearly the whole county is included. These extensions of the Green Belt draw attention to the great scale and persistent threat of urban sprawl. It became just as necessary in the 1970s to restrict building in the outer areas of Surrey as it did on the side nearest to London 20 years earlier. Only the Green Belt concept saved Surrey from being just a vast commuter dormitory. The very real danger of unplanned building development spreading like a scourge across the face of Surrey is illustrated by the proposal of the Guildford Rural District Council, successfully opposed by the Council for the Preservation of Rural England, to acquire in 1946 land for building below the famous viewpoint of Newlands Corner which fortunately still remains a purely rural landscape of great distinction. Another proposal successfully resisted was the London County Council's plan in 1948 to expand the population of the village of Westcott, near Dorking, to a town of some seven thousand. The county's *Structure Plan* (1977), now under public discussion, reaffirms the pivotal importance of the Green Belt concept in the fight against wholesale disfigurement and suggests proposals which will mitigate the effects of the competing claims on land in Surrey, so conserving the traditional well-cared-for countryside of pinewoods and copses, village greens, heather-covered hills, and small towns, and some of the finest old

121

red-brick and half-timbered cottages that it is possible to find in any county (Map 12, p. 120).

As much of Surrey and other sectors of Greater London have become more and more suburbanised since the turn of this century, inner London, including the part once Surrey, has decayed in the process of rehousing its population in new and expanding towns, and has led to destruction rather than renewal. G. K. Chesterton's stirring call in *The Buried City* (1932)

> 'You that dig up dead towns—arise and strive:
> Strike through the slums and raise the towns alive!'

A Surrey mower (1904)

has unhappily created not healthy, living, townships, but deserted urban hollows and dead towns. This urban environment and the green debateable land stretching between it and the coast offers one of the starkest constrasts of wealth and poverty, privilege and deprivation in modern Britain. From parts of inner London, in growing danger of becoming a divided plural society, 'the Green Belt looks like an unnatractive barrier of privilege protecting the interests of the very small number of residents who happen to live within it'. It has recently been wisely said that the Green Belt should be increasingly seen not as a sanctuary protecting the residents of rural Surrey against the masses of Londoners, but as protecting land for Londoners' recreation. In the fulfilment of this principle, Metropolitan Man's elemental response to the Surrey landscape in the 21st century will be the same as that of the landowning few in the 11th century. Now that we can all enjoy something like the pleasures experienced for centuries by the very rich, we must ensure that rural Surrey remains a pleasant place for living and working in, as well as for enjoying well-earned holidays, and not merely a kind of folk museum in which tomorrow's frustrated Londoners amuse themselves on Sundays.

Despite all the conspicuous damage it has suffered, unquestionably some of the worst near London, Surrey still retains many of the pleasing associations of its historic past. This is the reward of centuries of devotion, good taste, and also, it should be added, of money. We who have inherited this now precarious rural scene, once a scene of properly integrated and carefully looked after country estates, need to learn how the good landowner managed them and, in particular, how he maintained the necessary balance between beauty and function which still lends a distinctive but fast fading character to the sensitive and subtle landscape that is Surrey's.

Bibliography

The publications of the Surrey Archaeological Society (founded in 1854) comprise 120 volumes of the *Collections*, and a number of important Research Papers (two series). The Surrey Record Society has published 28 volumes of transcribed documents. An extensive use of these publications has been made in this *History* which it is not possible to list here.

The main collections of original documents relating to Surrey are deposited in the Surrey County Council Record Offices at Kingston and Guildford and also at the Minet Library, Brixton. The Library of the London Boroughs of Richmond-upon-Thames, Southwark and Wimbledon, amongst others, have important collections of source material. The muniments of Merton College, Oxford relating to its medieval Surrey manors of Chessington, Farleigh, Leatherhead and Old Malden are important. These collections have been considerably drawn upon for this *History*. The main class of documents utilised in the Public Record Office, Chancery Lane, has been the *Inquisitiones Post Mortem* (1272-1340). As the citation of references in the text is impracticable in this book the main original sources used are indicated, by subject, at the end of this Bibliography. Of the landscape artists and water colourists mentioned, John Linnell is represented by collections at the Tate Gallery, and London Museum and also at the City of Birmingham and Manchester Galleries; the largest collection of Samuel Palmer's works is at the Ashmolean Museum, Oxford; J. W. M. Turner's sketchbooks are in the Department of Drawings and Prints of the British Museum. The Fitzwilliam Museum, Cambridge, contains important 17th century paintings of Richmond-upon-Thames.

(N.B. Books cited in the text are not included in the Bibliography.)

John Aubrey, *The Natural History and Antiquities of the County of Surrey* (1718-19; reprinted, 1975)
Reginald Blomfield, *Richard Norman Shaw, R.A.* (1940).
F. R. H. du Boulay, *The Lordship of Canterbury* (1966).
E. W. Brayley, *History of Surrey* (5 vols., 1850).
Richard Brown, *Domestic Architecture* (1841).
E. R. Chamberlin, *Biography of Guildford* (1970).
Basil E. Cracknell, *Portrait of Surrey* (1974).
C. L. Cline (ed.), *The Letters of George Meredith* (1970).
W. Cobbett, *Rural Rides* (ed. G. D. H. and Margaret Cole) (1930).
Charles Cornish, *Wild England Today* (1900).
K. Courlander, *Richmond* (1953).
Daniel Defoe, *A Tour Through Great Britain* (1738 edition).
V. I. Evison, *The Fifth-Century Invasions South of the Thames* (1965).
Philip Gibbs, *England Speaks* (1936) (Sections IV and V contain much on Surrey between the Wars).
H. L. Gray, *English Field Systems* (1915).
J. E. B. Gover, A. Mawer and F. M. Stenton, *The Place-Names of Surrey*, English Place Name Society, volume XI (1934).
A. D. Hall and E. J. Russell, *Agriculture and Soils of Kent, Surrey and Sussex* (1911).
W. G. Hoskins, *The Making of the English Landscape* (1977 edition).
Wilfrid Hooper, *Reigate: Its Story Through the Ages* (1945).
Christopher Hussey, *English Gardens and Landscapes, 1700-1750* (1967).
M. B. Huish, *Happy England as painted by Mrs. Allingham* (1892) *Birket Foster* (1890).
Hugh Kenyon, *The Wealden Glass Industry* (1967).

Francis Jekyll, *Gertrude Jekyll* (1934).

Gertrude Jekyll, *Wood and Garden* (1899).

R. F. Jessup, *The Archaeology of South-East England* (1970).

H. M. Lloyd, 'Surrey', in *Domesday Geography of South-East England*, ed. H. C. Darby and E. M. J. Campbell (1962).

James Loudon, *An Encyclopaedia of Gardening* (1826). *Cottage Farm and Villa Architecture* (1857). *Country Residences* (   ).

M. Mack, *The Garden and the City* (1969).

Elfrida Manning, *Saxon Farnham* (1970).

O. Manning and W. Bray, *The History and Antiquities of Surrey* (1814, reprint 1974).

James Malcolm, *A Compendium of Modern Husbandry* (1805).

I. D. Margary, *Roman Ways in the Weald* (1948).

Anne Marsh, *Heathside Farm* (1863). (A novel set in west Surrey).

W. Marshall, *The Economy of the Southern Counties* (1798).

R. T. Mason, *Framed Buildings in the Weald* (1964).

Betty Massingham, *Miss Jekyll: A Portrait of a Great Gardener* (1966).

John R. Morris, *The Age of Arthur* (1973).

Ian Nairn and Nikolaus Pevsner, *The Buildings of England: Surrey* (2nd ed. 1971).

H. V. S. and Margaret Ogden, *English Taste in Landscape in the Seventeenth Century* (Ann Arbor, 1935).

Eric Parker, *Highways and Byways in Surrey* (1909 edition).

E. Pollard, M. D Hooper and N. W. Moore, *Hedges* (1974).

W. F. Rankine, *The Mesolithic of South England*. Surrey Archaeological Research paper, No. 4 (1956).

Peter J. Reynolds, Cambridge Introduction to the History of Mankind: *Farming in the Iron Age* (1976).

William Robinson, *The Wild Garden* (1870 edition).

John E. Salmon (ed.), *The Surrey Countryside: The Interplay of Land and People*. (British Association, 1975).

E. Straker, *Wealden Iron* (1931).

D. Stroud, *Capability Brown* (1954), *Humphry Repton* (1962).

S. Switzer, *Ichnographia Rustica* (1742 edition).

N. Temple, *Farnham Buildings and People* (1972 edition).

Victoria History of the counties of England: *Surrey* vols. 1-4 (1902-12).

P. A. L. Vine, *London's Lost Route to the Sea* (1965).

C. E. Vulliamy, *The Onslow Family, 1528-1874* (1953).

H. G. Wells, *Mr. Britling Sees it Through* (1916).

Rev. Gilbert White, *The Natural History and Antiquities of Selborne* (1826 edition).

S. W. Wooldridge and F. Goldring, *The Weald* (1953).

References to Original Sources

Guildford Muniment Room: Loseley Mss. 637, 729, 757, 955/1/2, 154/1—42. (Guildford Cloth-making).

Surrey County Record Office, Kingston: 329/13/1-4, 14/1-2 (18th century agriculture).

Minet Library, Brixton: 592 (Lambeth), 1574 (Camberwell), 2846-50, 2854, 6, 8 (Portnall, Egham), 3606 (medieval hunting), 3618 (Tandridge Priory), 3764 (Merton weaving).

Public Record Office, London: *Inquisitiones post mortem*; Ministers Accounts, Surrey; Forest Account, Surrey; Hearth Tax returns.

Victoria and Albert Museum Mss: H.34 (Thames-side landscape).

British Library: interleaved copy of Manning and Bray, *History and antiquities of Surrey* (1847), 30 vols.

Wimbledon Reference Library: interleaved Brayley, *History of Surrey* (5 vols.).

Minet Library: Collection of Drawings and Prints.

Index